Main Character Energy

FATS TIMBO

Main Character Energy

TEN COMMANDMENTS

For Living Life Fearlessly

BLINK
bringing you closer

First published in the UK by Blink Publishing
An imprint of Bonnier Books UK
4th Floor, Victoria House, Bloomsbury Square,
London, WC1B 4DA
Owned by Bonnier Books
Sveavägen 56, Stockholm, Sweden

Hardback – 978-1-788708-49-4
Ebook – 978-1-788708-51-7
Audio – 978-1-788708-52-4

A CIP catalogue of this book is available from the British Library.

Designed by EnvyDesignLtd
Printed and bound by Clays Ltd, Elcograf S.p.A.

1 3 5 7 9 10 8 6 4 2

Blink Publishing is an imprint of Bonnier Books UK
www.bonnierbooks.co.uk

Contents

To my parents Rugiatu and Amadu Timbo

Introduction

to the

Commandments

You want to live life your way. You want to be the main character in your story and you and I both know that takes some serious energy. So I'm here to step in with a helping hand. You see, in my short life, I've had more than enough experience of people trying to halt my main character flow – to make me into a supporting cast member or a comedy turn, a part of someone else's backstory or just some throwaway line. I've had to take care to develop the self-belief I need to be the hero in my own story and use it to turn my main character energy into a renewable resource (like the sun, for my international readers, or the wind and rain for those in the UK).

So first, what is main character energy? For me, it is about empowerment. The power to know that your dreams aren't secondary to other people's expectations. To see your goals as heroic, no matter how small they may seem to anyone else. The power to narrate your life in your own way, to direct your own story and determine your own course with the pride and self-belief that comes with knowing that you are the hero that your story needs.

I understand, though, that it can be hard to narrate your own life when there are so many other voices trying to drown yours out, to chart your own course when so many other people want to determine your direction, or to meet your own expectations when other people want you to live within theirs. So I've decided to share the lessons I've learned which help me overcome the doubts and doubters, the thoughts that give me that swell of inspiring main character music to get me through a low and a baseline for my mental montage when I'm building towards my next goal.

I've called these lessons commandments. I know that is a strong word. I am not really commanding you to do anything, but ten *suggestions* for living life fearlessly lacks a bit of punch, don't you think? I'm certain that *Significant Character Feelings: Ten mild encouragements to be a little less afraid* just wouldn't work. So I chose 'commandments' because these are more than suggestions. They are deeper than that. They can be applied by all of us, whenever we need them and wherever we are, because with them, our lives and the lives of others will be improved.

If you want to understand how I am using the idea of commandments, think about how you speak to your true friends when you need to give them honest advice – you stop tiptoeing around with suggestions and speak in commandments. We say things like, *You have to apply for that promotion, girl!* or, *You need to believe in yourself.* We move to commandments because we are telling them something that they already know is true but they either need a push to act on it or a reminder to believe in themselves. Most often, that thing is themselves and sometimes we all need to be commanded to believe in ourselves. So I am commanding you to believe in yourself, in the same way that I believe in these commandments.

I genuinely try to live by each and every one of these messages, even when some are harder to stick to than others. I see continuity and similarities between them and, even though some take love and others discipline, some a thousand small changes and others one big step, I believe that they all share a transformative power which will make your life easier to enjoy and bring your dreams within reach.

Some will at times be hard to live by, though. Our challenges are as unique as we are and depending on your situation and your personality, you will find some easier to take on board while others will require you to stop and think. Don't worry, though, because that is a great thing. Stopping and thinking (preferably in the rain with a cool backdrop and some epic tune) is key to retaining our main character energy and it is far better than living life on autopilot, continuing forward without considering what you believe or truly want. Because the lessons you struggle with are the ones that will make you grow. You will learn from them and they will form the basis of your commandments, helping you win your battles as the hero of your own story.

Before we begin, have a look at the commandments on the contents page. Stop and think about which of them you feel comfortable with right now, that you already live by, and mark down those where you feel like there is room to grow. When we get to the end of our time together, have a think about whether that has changed and see how you have grown, because knowing our challenges and appreciating ourselves when we confront them is key to self-love, to keeping our doubts at bay and our main character energy topped up.

Now you've done that, let's begin. The lights have dimmed and the music has stopped. My story is about to start and your journey is just beginning.

STOPPING AND THINKING (PREFERABLY IN THE RAIN WITH A COOL BACKDROP AND SOME EPIC TUNE) IS KEY TO RETAINING OUR MAIN CHARACTER ENERGY.

IT IS FAR BETTER THAN LIVING LIFE ON AUTOPILOT, CONTINUING FORWARD WITHOUT CONSIDERING WHAT YOU BELIEVE OR TRULY WANT.

COMMANDMENT 1:

Be Unexpected

Don't change yourself to fit the world's expectations, change the world to make it expect you.

People are always drawn to the unexpected. It's why we love magic shows and detective stories. It's the key to a good punchline and the reason we like to cheer for the underdog. It is also why people stare at others who seem different. I know what it's like to seem different, to have people stare, and I know what it is like to be unexpected. I guess, in that way, you could call this book, and my life, an underdog story – but you'd be wrong. It's so much more than that. It's a comedy, a tragedy and a tale of discovery. It's a manifesto for fearlessness and a guide to the magic of making the world accept the unexpected.

What would life be if it always matched our expectations? I'll answer that one for you. It would be *BORING*. The detective in the story would discover that the murderer was the man who walked around with the knife. Knock-knock jokes would all end with things like, 'Who's there?' . . .

'It's Mum, I forgot my keys' or 'Amazon delivery, you really need to stop buying scented candles.' There'd be no surprises and very few laughs, so, if I have a choice, I'll take a life of the unexpected every time.

I never really did have a choice, though – I guess you could say that the unexpected life chose me. No one expects someone to be four foot in high heels and they certainly don't expect that person to be twerking on a police car. (OK, maybe that part was my choice. I'll explain later.) The truth is, no one saw me coming and they still don't. So if people are going to stare, I'll have to give them a good reason to. I'll try to be stared at for the same reason the magician is when they reveal their trick or comedians are when we drop a great punchline – because when you defy expectations, people's eyes are drawn to you.

Accepting myself and my situation has not always been easy, though, and through this book you'll see I'm still learning. There are still moments when the unwanted attention and the unshakeable sense of my own difference is too much, but, even so, I have grown to love a life of the unexpected. I hope the lessons I have learned in the process can help you, because I think they are universal.

We all worry about being different sometimes and yet at the same time, all of us want to feel special, which is a contradiction. We want to fit in and we all want to stand out, and that's enough to make anyone confused. Well, I think I can help with that confusion. I think I can show you how to be one in a million. Where everyone in that million is unique in their way but most are hiding it for fear of being unexpected. The easy part is that you don't have to change yourself and the fun part is that you've got to change the world.

So let me tell you a bit about myself, about the ways in which I'm outside people's expectations, about the things that I haven't changed and I've learned to accept, and then later we can get on to the whole changing the world part . . .

I'm Fats/Fatima. I'm a comedian; I make jokes and videos. Sometimes I go on news programmes and tell men with bad tans what life is like for little people. I do this because I am a little person, in case you were wondering. Doing that on the news would be a bit odd if I wasn't. Being a little person, or having achondroplasia (if you are practising for a spelling bee), doesn't define me but it's definitely a part of my experience that has refined me. It's one of the forces in my life that has shaped how

I respond to the world because it has shaped how the world responds to me. It is the reason that I have got used to being unexpected and learned not to be afraid of that fact. Most of the time, anyway.

So I'll take you back to the beginning, back to the moment when my parents had their *what not to expect when you're expecting* moment, because all good underdog stories start around birth, and no magic trick can be understood if you join in the middle.

Six months into her pregnancy, my mum, Rugiatu, was called into the hospital by the pregnancy specialist. She found herself in a grey-green waiting room, the likes of which she has come to know very well in the years since. She knew that doctors rarely call expectant mothers into hospital at six months just to tell them random good news because the good things about people are very rarely visible on scans. Difficult things are what scans are for. So she was nervous, even though that's not her personality type. In fact, she is a very positive person, but any of you who have gone through pregnancy probably know better than I do that no amount of positivity is enough to overcome the hope and fear that come with it. My dad, Amadu, just sat beside her and held her hand; it was all he could do.

They entered the doctor's office and listened to him speak in that voice that doctors learn to do. One that has had all of the hope and fear removed because there is enough of that going round on the ward. He said the scan showed I wasn't growing at the normal rate and that my head was growing faster than my body. It was unexpected. My mum asked what it meant, whether it was a sign that she was going to lose the small person inside her that she felt she already knew. The doctor said he couldn't confirm anything. When you are talking to fearful and hopeful people it is best not to make assumptions, but he said there were two conditions associated with that kind of foetal development – dwarfism and Down's syndrome – and that it was very likely I would be born with one of them. He offered her a termination.

My mum didn't take it. She listened to her body and looked at her circumstances and knew she was comfortable with her choice. I was to be unexpected and I was to be loved and appreciated beyond all imagination. My parents had learned to love and expect the unexpected.

They had to learn even faster once I was born. Long before I was adapting the world and making it adapt to me, they began making adaptations of their own. I had to have surgery on my ears every year, as children with dwarfism often have fluid on the brain which can travel down to the ears and leave us Deaf. For the first five years of my life, I had to have steroid injections in my legs every day to help me grow. My parents were meticulous, going everywhere prepared with a little travel bag of syringes, as if they were proper intense bodybuilders. In a way that's not a bad description of them: *intense body builders*. It was intense and they helped to build my body. I tried to help in my own way – my dad tells me that after a couple of years, I began to call out, 'Daddy, it's injection time,' down the hallway each evening as I ran to him in the sitting room. I had become used to the challenges I faced and the expectation of a life filled with doctor's visits. In fact, I just thought it was because I was a *very* special little girl and so the doctors wanted to see me more than anyone else.

If it sounds like my parents and I were somehow better placed than most to deal with the unexpected, I think you might be right. They have an ability to embrace situations and they taught me to face mistakes with a smile on my face too. In 2018, on the way back from a holiday in Tenerife, we arrived at the check-in desk to be told that our flight had left *the day before*. We just burst out laughing. It started with my mum but then it was all of us. Like, proper belly laughing, and as soon as one of us managed to stop, another set the others off again. If you want to know my family and how we respond to adversity, that's a pretty good example. My approach to life and my decision to go into comedy probably comes from my parents and that attitude of theirs. They don't take anything too seriously, they are jokers, and no amount of syringes and doctor's appointments was ever going to be enough to stop us laughing. My family taught me that if you can laugh, you'll always be fine.

My parents still laugh when they tell the story of how they met. I bet in someone else's biography it would be told as a sad story. They arrived in the UK from Sierra Leone around the time of the civil war and were both working as cleaners in a hotel. My dad mentioned that he was missing his traditional food and my mum offered to cook for him. She went over to cook one meal and stayed for *30 years*. The truth was that she had nowhere else to go but she backed her stew to get her a pass to stay. I think that's just another example of how my parents see the world. You could hear that story and notice the hard parts – the war, the low wage work, not having a place to stay – but when my mum tells it she smiles. For her, it's a happy tale – a love story, a great review of her cooking and another example of how she managed to make life work out her way by smiling and sticking with it.

Maybe you could call our family's tendency to laugh in the face of difficult situations an adaptation or maybe you would call it perspective. I think you can only see adaptations for what they are once you have a chance to look back, because when you are in the moment, you are just acting on instinct. That was definitely the case for me as a child, learning to work with a world that wasn't built for someone my size. I couldn't reach any of the light switches in our house, so I developed all of these wild little modifications to make it possible. In the corridor, I found that I could press my back to the wall, put my feet and hands on the opposite side and climb up, one foot and one hand at a time until I was high enough to reach the light switch. In the bathroom, I had a similar move but sideways, where I would jump like a starfish and catch myself – hands and legs outstretched – between the two walls. Then I would basically walk myself up until I could flick the switch. Every day was like an episode of *Ninja Warrior* in my toilet, but the only prize at the end was turning on a light. I think most contestants on the show would be disappointed when they reached the end of *that* course . . . Some other moves in my repertoire were simpler: getting a plate was just a matter of climbing on the counter tops and getting into bed just required a little jump. It wasn't all Spider-Girl stuff but, looking back, I do wonder how I had the strength and flexibility for some of those moves. Small children are incredible athletes.

Of course, my athletic ability only extended to certain moves, so primary school sports day didn't usually end with a great medal haul. In year one, I remember being at the starting line of the running race, adrenaline pumping, prepared to give it my best shot, and then that feeling of watching everyone else shoot off into the distance. The harder and faster I tried to run, the greater the gap between me and the other kids seemed to grow. I remember asking *why*? The sense of unfairness hit me in a way it didn't when I fought to reach a light switch or clambered for a plate. I could overcome my limitations in those situations with thought and effort, but no matter how hard I tried, I could never be as fast as the other kids in my class. I just wanted to be able to compete with everyone else on fair terms, but I quickly saw that it wouldn't be possible – so I would have to take a different approach and live by my own standards. I realised that I can't live my life comparing myself to others – and that actually, I don't think anyone should. I learned to compete only with myself, to be better than I was the last time I tried something – to reach higher light switches and jump on to bigger beds.

I think that is a useful life lesson for all of us: don't base your expectations of yourself on the actions of others because it leaves too much outside of your own control. I think that's why I grew to love dancing. In dance, it's not about how strong or fast your body is but how you use it. As an unexpected person, with a body that is different to most, I am very lucky to pursue a life that is creative rather than competitive because in the world of creation and collaboration, the unexpected is *essential*.

I started dancing as soon as I could move but my parents say the breakthrough moment came when I was five years old. We were at a big family party, with more uncles and aunts than you can imagine, and music blaring over the speaker system like it always did. When I heard it, I took a few steps away from my parents and started to throw some shapes. In my mind, what I was doing was perfectly normal, the natural response to a good tune and a hardwood floor, but everyone stopped and stared. In a film, it would have been that classic moment where one person drops their drink and another spits theirs out in shock, because apparently the whole room stopped to watch me go. Here I was being unexpected again, and the extended family couldn't get enough. My auntie even snapped a photo and put it in a magazine that she was running at the time. My parents acted quickly when they saw how happy it made me, enrolling me in a dance school near our home in East Ham. I started doing jazz, tap, ballet, acrobatics and I loved every last minute of it. It was a time when everything felt possible inside my body and everything became calm in my mind.

After a few months at dance school, I was cast in my first role in the musical *Cats*. I must have been a strange cat as my main goal in performing was to show off how flexible I was – picture more of a feline Pilates instructor than a musical theatre star (though I would argue that cats generally value flexibility more than jazz hands, so the portrayal was accurate). When showtime approached, I had a similar feeling to the one I had back on the starting line at sports day, with coiled-up energy and excitement that made me feel ready to burst. But I could also tell it was different. I wasn't there to beat anyone and the skill that the other dancers showed could only make me look better. We were collaborating, not competing, and that felt right. Then again, the first thing I did when I walked out was wave at my mum and dad with a toothy five-year-old's grin on my face, so I can't pretend it was an entirely selfless moment.

Then we began to dance. I put my legs behind my head. I jived and shimmied and threw all kinds of shapes and the crowd went wild. I had never felt anything like the sensation that the crowd's applause brought up in me; any feelings of fear and anticipation transformed into adrenaline and endorphins as I heard them roar. It was the most satisfying feeling I had ever experienced. If I'm honest, it was probably quite a small crowd, politely clapping as small children did their best to perform routines that they had practised really hard, but to me that didn't matter. In my mind, I was on Broadway, the seats extended 200 feet up into the auditorium and roses were being thrown on to the stage. Somewhere, a reporter with a notepad in the brim of their hat was writing about the small cat who had brought together dance and gymnastics in a way that Plaistow had never seen before.

BE UNEXPECTED

In my mind and in my legs, which bore all the marks of their rejections and injections, I knew I was on the road to stardom. I was going to be an entertainer. Even if it was the last thing everyone expected.

What you'll find next is the first The Timbo Takeaway. I know that sounds like a Sierra Leonean restaurant but actually it's a summary of the main lessons from the chapter that it follows. The Takeaways are designed so that you can always dip back into this book for a quick reminder of its key messages, even when time is tight and you are too busy crusading on your main character quest to re-read a whole chapter.

Afterwards, I've included some questions and space for reflections you might have. Take a moment to think about how the commandments fit with your life and use the questions as a springboard to help you understand your perspectives and goals in a new way – because this book is as much about you as it is about me. It's just a crossover where the main character from my story interacts with the main character from yours. Think *Avengers*, or *Godzilla vs. Kong* but with fewer explosions and a lot more love.

The Timbo Takeaway

There will be times in your life when you feel different to the rest, like you stand out, like some people don't want you to fit in. Ask yourself whether a life fitting in is what you really want. Do the people you admire choose to fit in, to blend among the sea of faces? Or do they accept that they will have to be seen to make a change, that they will have to defy people's expectations if they are to raise them?

If we are to be seen and heard, we have to recognise that some people will stare and others will choose not to listen. So we have to accept the things we cannot change and then focus on those that we can – while appreciating how our adversaries help to mould us as much as our supporters do. When we have done that it is down to us to find the things in life that give us meaning and make our lives valuable on our own terms.

Because living outside of others' expectations means living by our own rules, and those rules are yours to discover. So consider what makes your life feel meaningful, what makes your heart sing, and what forms the basis of your expectations – free from the pressures of everyone else's. Who knows, as you defy the expectations of others, you might find you even outdo your own.

Reflections

What are the things I want to achieve?

....
....
....
....

What are the challenges I might face when I defy people's expectations?

....
....
....
....

How could those challenges help me to grow?

....
....
....
....

Come back to this section the next time you are chasing a dream or facing a challenge and remind yourself that sometimes the hard times take us further than the easy ones.

I WAS TO BE UNEXPECTED AND I WAS TO BE LOVED AND APPRECIATED BEYOND ALL IMAGINATION.

COMMANDMENT 2:

Let Love

Be Your

Superpower

Take care of those who care about you and they will help you to fly.

TIMBO FAMILY TREE

Rugiatu Timbo   Amadu Timbo

Lizzie	Mbarlu	Fatima	Abdul	Sentou
(b.1987)	(b.1991)	(b.1997)	(b.1997)	(b.2000)

I'm not one to blow my own trumpet (actually, who am I kidding? I'm great and so are you, so let's start a self-love brass band) but my title for this chapter should really be a song too. I reckon it would be one of those eighties ballads, all big hair and big emotions, sung by a woman in a cape with lots of fierce make-up.

Love is your superpower,
One million miles per hour,
Raise me up to your tower,
Of looooooooooooove . . .

Obviously, I will be standing on top of a tower as I perform this hit and my guitar will most likely shoot rays of love that could have ended the Cold War (#maincharacterenergy). I'm sure you can see it now – it's a work in progress, but aren't we all?

In my experience, the best people to understand that idea – that we are a work in progress – are our family and friends. It's because they are the ones who have been with us and will be with us for the long haul. Their perspective allows them to see us in more dimensions than just the present, with an understanding of the people that we have always been and the ones that we can become. Their appreciation of the variables and constants of our personalities through highs and lows allows them to speak to us with a more powerful honesty and a deeper sense of our potential than most. They can advise us and forgive us in a way that others might not be able to. And all this is just part of the reason that I believe the commandment 'take care of those who care for us' to be a worthy one.

I should say, first of all, that when I use the word 'family' here, I don't necessarily mean a biological one. Your family may be adopted or chosen, and in my eyes that doesn't change the relationship; if you feel like family then you are a family, and even on those days when you *don't*, well, you're in it for the long haul. The idea of extended family beyond the biological is actually quite typical in Sierra Leonean culture and African cultures more widely. If you asked me how many aunties I have, there would be two answers: one would be the sum total of my mum's and dad's sisters and the other would be about 263, as any woman with a deep connection to my family qualifies as an auntie in Sierra Leonean culture. I think that's a great thing because the more people who are there for us in the hard times, and the more people we can be there for in return, the better.

It makes us stronger to know we have a support network and less fearful of taking leaps if the safety net they provide is wide. When I wanted to leave my professional life as an accountant (yes, I was an accountant and I know what you're thinking, it was *so* not me, but more about that later) it was one of the aunties I spoke about who convinced my dad not to be afraid of the risk I was taking. She was able to speak on my behalf and reassure him that I could succeed on a path that looked strange and precarious to him. She was considered a part of my family, so she was able to influence that pivotal decision.

When I think about my dad's life, I understand why he would want me to have a certain level of professional security. It's not just about the African parent stereotype of wanting your child to have a serious career (see: doctor, lawyer, accountant. Do not see: TikTok comedian, animator, DJ), it's a reflection of his life experience. For him, stability and security are not things to be taken for granted, and qualifications are not something that many people in the world are able to access. His efforts to secure qualifications took him from Sierra Leone to Moscow after finishing school and from there on to Uzbekistan.

I think that it was quite a culture shock for a boy from Freetown, Sierra Leone's capital. He went from Moscow to Soviet-era Uzbekistan to gain a qualification in agriculture science and hated it, but he knew that as a person from a poorer nation who wanted to succeed in a globalising world, he would need qualifications. The plan changed because he spent his holidays visiting family and friends in London, and the appeal of living in the UK became too great, so he gave up on agriculture to try to start again in England. London was just so attractive for him – a land of opportunity with a thriving Sierra Leonean community and an optimism that the

USSR just didn't have at the time. I guess his love of Sierra Leonean people and friends led him, and as that's the message of this commandment I can't fault him for his choice, even though I know it would have been hard to leave the security of the pathway he was on to start again. Maybe that experience of changing his life plans and choosing a path of less security in exchange for greater happiness influenced his decision to support me when I did the same.

He actually wanted to retrain as a doctor when he arrived in London, but it was too expensive and time-consuming. He had to support himself in an expensive city and the jobs he could work at that time just wouldn't fund a medical degree. So I understand why he doesn't take qualifications for granted, even though he accepted me when I made my career change into a world with less security. Thinking about his life for this book has helped me to realise that about him and to better understand his approach to our conversations when I wanted to leave accountancy for creativity. I take that as another example of why we should take care of those who care for us, because caring requires us to listen, and by listening we learn – both about those we are listening to and about ourselves.

He did end up working in healthcare, though,

as he retrained as a mental health nurse. In the early 1990s, the British government made a big push to get more people qualified and although he didn't think nursing would be for him initially, he grew to love it. Helping people to improve their mental health has been pivotal in his life and has had a big impact on how he has supported me all through my life. He has seen how important it is to take care of your mind and how having a secure sense of self is at the root of everything else we do. He was able to tell me with complete confidence that even with all of my physical limitations (no competitive basketball for me!), if I could be happy and feel mentally secure, then I would be able to flourish.

His dedication to helping people with mental health challenges even took him back to Sierra Leone as an expert when he helped to develop the one psychiatric hospital in the country. He says it used to be a very dark place, somewhere that no one would want to leave a family member, but, in part because of the role he has played, it has become a modern medical facility which treats lots of patients and performs outreach to change the perception of mental illness in Sierra Leone, which is amazing.

When he first went back with his goal of modernising the mental health system in 2014, he met the minister for health and asked him when he had last visited the hospital. The minister told him that he had never been. Fast-forward a few years and it is not just ministers who have visited but the president himself, who cut the ribbon on the new building after it was refurbished. I know my dad is really proud of that, that he returned to his home to try to improve people's lives, and I know that it was love that gave him the power to do it.

I think that my dad's attitude and the path he took reflects the energy that characterises my family – take your goals seriously but don't let them weigh you down. Plans will change, some things may go wrong, but you have to stay positive and keep moving forward. I see that outlook in myself and all my family members – a funny mixture of resilience and playfulness that allows us to enjoy the good times and still laugh in the bad. It is what gives me perspective in the moments where I feel hard done by and a belief in the possibility of better times when I feel out of luck.

The other characteristic that I think defines my family is care, which is one of the reasons I have made it the focus of this chapter. You've seen how my dad dedicated his life to a caring profession, but my mum and older sister have done the same. My mum is a nurse and, while I was growing up, she would spend long days at the hospital taking care of sick people and then return home to do the same for us. I honestly can't get my head around that level of dedication. She tells me that I will understand it someday and I hope I will, but I also wouldn't mind just a little bit more downtime than she ever managed! I guess it is a feature of her personality to be caring, a reflex rather than a choice which means she acts to help before thinking about why. If someone needs help then my mum is already helping. Sometimes before they even say it, before they even know that they need help themselves.

My sister Lizzie is the same. If love is a super-power then she should be leading the Avengers because caring is just in her nature. After my parents, she was my most important role model growing up. She is ten years older than me and sometimes feels like a second parent. When my mum was working, she would take care of me, my younger brother and sister, and I owe her so much for that. It is only as I have got older that I have realised the sacrifices she made for us. As a teenager, she would often turn down offers from her friends to go out because she had to support us, and even in her adult life she decided to live close to our home to be there for her siblings. To this day, she continues to give us love and affection when we need it the most, so it is no surprise that she became a social worker, and an amazing one as well. It is almost like she had an apprenticeship before she started her career. So when she was done helping us all through hard times she stepped into the world of work and hit the ground running. It makes me feel so happy to know there are people like my big sister out there giving help to those who need it, and thankfully, she doesn't make me feel silly for dedicating my life to the less serious pursuit of making people laugh.

I didn't know my other older sister, Balu, when I was growing up. There were challenges for her coming to the UK, so she lived with my grandma in Sierra Leone until she was 18 and I was ten. As soon as I met her though, I knew she was special. Trust me, she's the real comedian in the family and has this amazing ability to turn any situation into a joke. She's also a really independent woman and I love that. I think it's because she experienced those two lives, growing up in Sierra Leone and then moving to the UK, so she had to develop her independence early to help make that transition. Now she lives in the US with her husband and five children in a beautiful home with this huge, landscaped garden that covers over with frost every winter. We visit her and she comes over to London every year or so which keeps us close, and I always know we are going to have a good time when Balu's about.

My two younger siblings are closer in age to me and there is a different dynamic than with my older sisters because we've grown up together. First, there is my brother Abdul, who is only ten months younger than me. He's a very laid-back guy, to the point that if they ever started a political party in favour of relaxation I'd put him forward to be its leader, even though I imagine he'd be too busy chilling to take the job. Trust me when I say that man can *chill. Indefinitely.* You could tell him there was a fire in the house and he'd probably just say 'Is it?' and slightly adjust his position on the couch to avoid the flames. Abdul enjoys life at his own pace and you can't deny that is a skill. He's a special person. Abdul was born three months premature. So when my parents were learning to support me in the first years of my life, they were given another mission to keep him alive and make him strong. It was hard and he had to fight for survival to the point where my dad says he didn't know whether to buy a cot or a coffin in those first few months. Abdul had to have a tracheotomy to help him breathe and eat as his windpipe didn't have the chance to fully develop when he was in the womb and he still bears the scars.

I sometimes wonder whether his appreciation for the easy life comes from experiencing that hardship as a baby or whether it's just his personality type. I think it's probably the latter because you don't become as chilled as my bro without having some kind of genetic predisposition to comfy chairs and an internal GPS locked on to the path of least resistance. Here is an example that illustrates his willingness to let madness rage around him with a peaceful smile on his face – it's both really not funny and quite funny. A few years ago, one of my brother's friends died. It was terrible, a beautiful young man lost too soon. Abdul went to the funeral home where the service was being given. He went in and took his seat only a few minutes late, which is not bad by his chilled standards.

A full 40 minutes later, he started wondering why they kept talking about his friend's long life. About his children. His husband. Abdul started to wonder whether he had missed a few crucial facts about this friend of his while they had been together. Then he looked up at the coffin. Instead of a picture of his friend he saw a photo of an elderly woman. He had gone into the wrong service and not noticed until it was almost over. He waited for the right moment and slipped out to the correct service, which was taking place next door. I'm *so* glad that he hadn't been asked to give the eulogy.

I've always felt the need to look out for him and I'm sure, if he was pressed, he'd say he feels the same about me. I know he's always there for me, even if it might take him a little while to get there. I feel a similar duty of care for my youngest sister, even if she doesn't seem to need it. That sister is Sentou and she is the definition of independence, an alternative Black girl who does things her own way. No clubs or hair salons for her: she wants to make art, read graphic novels and spend time with her close friends. She has sort of always had to go against the grain and defy expectations. When she was conceived my dad said, 'That's going to be five children now! It's going to be too many!' but obviously my mum shut that down. Although she does like to repeat the story. Every time we pass the restaurant where he said that to her, she reminds us. 'Hey, Sentou! That's where your dad complained about you being born!' (I told you my family takes the serious things lightly and light-hearted things more seriously . . .)

The drama escalated to another level when she was born. My mum says her labour with Sentou was the worst she has ever experienced. The deepest, sharpest pain that you can imagine. When they were in the delivery room she told my dad that it was too much, that she wasn't sure she could take it. He told her that as she'd already had four, she might be used to it by now. He basically said 'calm down'. Naturally, World War Three erupted. My mum demanded that security eject him from the hospital and that he be kept off the premises until she was done. Dad did as he was told but soon managed to convince the staff to let him back in to have another try at being supportive. Thankfully, it worked because as funny as it is that a man can be barred from the birth of his own child for rudeness, I hear meeting your newborn is sort of a big deal. Even if it is number five.

That story always makes my family laugh, even though it probably didn't seem vaguely funny at that moment. It reminds me to try to keep in mind that even the hardest things will probably somehow be funny to look back on one day. Here, you try it. Remind yourself of the worst boss or teacher you ever had. Think back to what it was like being around them, the frustration and loathing, and now think about the image of them that you have in your head. Unless it was a genuinely traumatic experience, they probably appear to you as just another character in the story of your life, part of your history that you can laugh about now with other people who knew them. That's what I mean when I say things that aren't fun can often be funny in hindsight.

Anyway, after my dad was allowed back into the hospital and into Sentou's life, she began to grow into one of the most brilliant people I know. Introverted, independent and creative, with a huge personality that she reveals to you when you've established her trust. She has just qualified as an animator and has her own TikTok and Insta channels (@smallpwbbles) where she shares her art which is doing really well. I love that she is following her own path, but I've always known she would, ever since she *ran away from home aged one*. Yes, I kid you not, her life was more dramatic between the years of minus one and one than most of ours are in the following twenty. I can still remember the day. My dad came home from work and went upstairs to speak to my mum. When he asked her where Sentou was she replied that she was in the sitting room. At the time, Mum was busy caring for Abdul, who had just come home from hospital, and making sure Spider-Girl didn't climb too far up the walls, so she didn't notice that the front door was open and Sentou was gone. I can picture it now, my sister toddling out of the door as if to say, 'Bye Felicia! I'm one and a half, I'm taking myself to the park.'

My parents obviously panicked, gathered us up and rushed out to find her. They looked up and down the road and then went over to the park just across from our house. Flustered, they asked anyone they could find whether they had seen an unaccompanied, er . . . *baby*. After a few tries, some people had the answer they were looking for. 'Yeah, we saw a kid. She seemed fine but we thought she was too young to be out on her own' – *yeah, just a bit* – 'so we called the police.' Now, people calling the police on your child isn't normally something you feel relieved about, but for my parents, it was good news. They rushed to the local police station with their hearts beating in their chests, carrying a little girl and a toddler with a tracheotomy. They didn't think of how they would prove that the baby was theirs once they got there; they just hoped she would be there. Fortunately, when they burst through the door, Sentou was sitting on a blue plastic chair, chanting 'Dad-dy, Dad-dy' as my dad ran in. The police believed the story, though they had to admit that it was a first, even in East Ham, to see a baby take themselves to the park. Social services also saw that it was just an honest mistake involving a very proactive child. If I hadn't been three I could have told them that Sentou just goes her own way. Always has, always will.

Unstoppable women (/babies) are a feature of my family. My grandmother is 94 and still moves around like she's in her twenties. She was shot in the leg during the war in Sierra Leone but that couldn't stop her and when we went to Sierra Leone for Balu's wedding in 2022, she was still running the show. Every day, we would head over to her house and there would be a spread laid out to feed at least 20 people – uncles, aunts, cousins, cousin's uncles and *aunt's friend's nephews* who had *maybe* once met my mum. I was introduced to half of Freetown on that trip over peanut or cassava leaf stew, and I still can't work out whether they were there to meet the English family over for the wedding or just to eat some of the best rice this side of the equator. My grandma makes the best rice and I don't think I am quite able to explain how important rice is in Sierra Leonean culture. I've talked to you about care and I've talked about family but this is the first mention of long grain, the last member of every Sierra Leonean family and the one which provides and receives the most love. Feeling sick? Have a bit of rice. Feeling good? Have a bit of rice. Unsure what you feel like? I reckon rice will do nicely. It's nourishment but it is also a show of love, and we take care of rice just like it has taken care of us. My grandma has been shot, seen war and independence struggles, and raised more children than the Dragon ride at Legoland, and it's rice that has been by her side every step of the way.

It is with that, dear friend, that I present my family — The Timbos. Baby-finding, funeral-swapping, rice-loving Londoners with one foot in Freetown and the other in East Ham. We fight and we laugh, we forgive and forget, and we remember that no matter what comes our way, we will always be there to care for one another. So, if you can, try to take care of the people who care about you. Even when they frustrate you or wind you up, even when you want them kicked out of the labour ward, remember that they are the people who will forgive you in your lowest moments and most appreciate the path you have scaled when you reach your heights. Their love is your superpower, and yours can be theirs.

Because even though we are all a work in progress, if we have learned to truly care for those who have cared for us, then our work is as good as done.

Grandma can be proud and you can too.

Rice, anyone?

The Timbo Takeaway

(I'll have the cassava leaf stew, please. Lol jk.)

Our family is anyone who truly knows us. They are the people that forgive our mistakes because they know we can do better and who celebrate our successes because they know where we've come from. Find your family and take care of them, because you never know when you will need more strength than you have alone, or how much love you have to give unless you stay close to those who need it.

Of course, being with family is not always good, but, even if it seems like it, it will not always be bad. Stick with those who are looking out for you and look out for them in return. You will be able to stretch out further in pursuit of your dreams if you know there are people who will catch you should you fall.

Reflections

Who is your family? Whether they are your relatives or not, what is it that binds you together?

Think of a time when your family frustrated you or asked you to do something that you did not feel like doing. Now try to think of why they might have done that, both from the perspective of what they needed and from the perspective of what they might have wanted for you.

What could you do this week to show your family love? Note it down and then try to do it.

....
....
....
....
....
....
....
....
....
....
....
....
....

PLANS WILL CHANGE, SOME THINGS MAY GO WRONG, BUT YOU HAVE TO STAY POSITIVE AND KEEP MOVING FORWARD.

Rise Above

Every great thing was at one point new and different. Those who fear their own difference will want to point out yours. So if you want to be great, you will need to rise above.

A difficult truth about living and thriving with main character energy is that the journey is often going to be hard. Every heroic story and epic journey needs challenges and opponents along the way otherwise there would be nothing heroic or epic about it at all. This commandment sums up probably the greatest challenge I have faced and so it's the one that I have found hardest to live by on my journey. It is a commandment that stands out from the others and for that I think it is even more powerful.

Why is that? Well, if you look through the list you will see that most start with you. Some call you to look at your ways of thinking and free yourself from fears and doubts, while others drive you to reach for the dreams that, deep down, you know you can grasp. But rising above? Blocking out the haters? That can be more difficult because in this case, the challenges you face begin elsewhere, with people who fear their own difference and want to make you fearful of yours. It is because there are aspects of this commandment beyond your control, like the anger that others feel, the relentlessness with which they direct it at you and the numbers in which they come, that it can feel harder to live by. So I understand that there will be times when all those things make it feel too hard to rise above the haters, that your lack of influence over the way others treat you makes it seem like their problem not yours. That last part is certainly true, but it is also true that their problem will become yours unless you have your own solutions. I hope you will see from my experiences that I describe in this chapter that you have more power than you realise in the face of bullies.

I say that because even when you experience the cruellest treatment, you do have power, because the one thing haters can never control is your response to them. Now, before you say it, I know it sounds like I'm telling you to just turn the other cheek and I know how frustrating a thing it can be to hear. If I had a pound for every time I've been told that words can never hurt me then my TikToks would be filmed from my own private island. (I think that content would do very well actually. Maybe I'll start a Patreon, for the good of my fans . . . you know?) But the problem is, it's true. It is simply, deeply and sometimes annoyingly true. Because even though having control of your own reactions may seem like a small thing when you're faced with cruelty, as you practise it, you find that it is more than just a reaction and more than just a shield against the nastiness of the fearful; it is a sword in its own right. Rising above the hate of others can be enough to defeat it and it can even turn those who choose cruelty into kinder people themselves. It's a magic mirror that shows the aggressive their own weakness and your stillness in a new light, as the true strength that it is.

I feel confident to tell you that because I have experienced enough bullying to last a lifetime, it has made me something of an expert in bullying bounce backs (BBBs). I'm going to tell you how I got here and how you can become fearless in the face of your haters if you're unfortunate enough to be stuck with some.

If you are in that position then I hope I can make you aware of the power you have within to overcome it, but equally, I want you to understand where else you can turn and how you can convert your internal strength into external support. I have always ignored haters up to a point, but at school when it was constant and when it amounted to bullying, I would always tell a teacher. My mother taught me that was the way to be, that no one had a right to bully her daughter. It took courage to speak up but I knew that there were adults around who could help sort it out. Because bullying is about bullies looking for power in a world where they feel powerless and, like it or not, if you are at school your teachers can try to combat that. They have the power to reach out to your bullies' parents, to take away privileges that your bully enjoys and to take control. It is the same in a workplace, even if the support structures are less clear. HR departments are there to support people who are having a difficult time and even if you don't want to raise a formal complaint, if you are struggling because of the way someone is treating you it is always better to get that out in the open. You have to find the courage to admit you need some help, but after that, it is up to other people to do their job and help you. I had one really bad bully when I was 15 at secondary school and I think the way that my story with him developed explains this point quite well. He hurt me and I didn't hide from my emotions, but it was my reaction to those emotions and my ability to rise above that made the difference in the long term.

This bully was vicious. He called me names every day, sought me out to get his daily fix of imaginary power and soon began sending me messages over the internet. He did it for two years. A few months in, I decided to stop seeing those messages as reflections of me but as reflections of him, and I started to treat them as evidence. I screenshotted every one, built up a case file for the prosecution and when I decided it was clear enough, that no one could deny that his messages amounted to sustained and dedicated attempts to hurt me, I printed them and gave them to our head of year. They dealt with it, which I think is the least you can expect. His family were contacted, his privileges were removed and the strength that he felt he had through secrecy was taken away when I showed his words to the world. People tell me that was a brave thing to do, and now when I look back at my younger self I see that it was, but back then, I just thought it was necessary. It was survival.

Now that same guy contacts me on social media to tell me how well I have done, how beautiful I am, how proud he is. I messaged back to ask him if he remembered bullying me and he just said that he had been young and didn't know any better. I didn't try to make him understand how he had made me feel. Maybe I should have, maybe I could have changed one person, but I had to think about my own wellbeing and I had to save my energy for bigger and better things.

The online world that we grew up in has changed the way that hate is spread. People talk about this a lot and I know there is a lot of research and evidence about how social media abuse and negative online communication can lead to mental health problems for teenagers, and in particular teenage girls. I see that. It is particularly difficult in those cases where people experience bullying from people that they would like to believe are their friends. My advice in that case is to know your worth and not to be afraid of stepping away from them. You have to know that anyone who brings you down is not worthy of being called your friend. Friendships are partnerships which make you both stronger. In any case where a friend finds strength in making you feel weak you should be prepared to cut them loose. That can seem difficult but believe me it needs to happen – there are other people and other friendships, so sticking with those that are built on cruelty will only hold you back from finding ones that are built on love. So if you have a friend who is constantly bringing you down, ask them why. If they can't answer you, or if they respond with anger and won't change their behaviour, you have to be brave enough to rise above and cut yourself loose, because you deserve better.

In the other case, if you have a bully you know who is attacking you online, like the boy I knew at secondary school, then follow my lead. One of the benefits of online communication is that everything can be stored, every cruel remark can be screenshotted and every attack saved as evidence. That didn't used to be the case, so for all that social media and the internet has made bullying easier and potentially a 'round the clock' activity, it has also made it easier to expose and to act on. Don't be afraid to screenshot and share with people who can help you. That is what I mean by rising above. Feel the hurt that person has caused you, understand that you don't deserve it and respond by rising above their methods: fighting fire with fire gets everyone burned, but being cool as ice and choosing to seek help allows you to put out the flame that your hater has lit.

Just don't bottle it up.

It is important to be conscious of the difference

between those who don't understand you and those who try to bring you down, though. I experience that lack of understanding with little kids every week of my life. They point, stare and ask questions, and that can be hard, but I've learned to see it for what it is. They are trying to understand the world, the similarities and differences between people, and as draining as it can be for me to be treated as one of the points of difference, I have to be strong and believe that they will soon accept without judgement. Sometimes I speak to their parents, though. I suggest they tell their children not to stare and to explain that bodies come in all shapes and sizes, which are of equal value regardless of their form. Sometimes I feel hurt. Sometimes I wish that I could be free of the attention for just one day, to walk through a shopping centre without people turning and looking at me, whispering, judging. Sometimes I feel like it is enough to break me down.

That happened on a day out this year. It all became too much and I sat on a bench beside a branch of The Body Shop and started to cry. I don't see that as a failure to rise above, though; I see that as a natural emotional response. When I say you have control of your own reactions, I don't mean that you shouldn't feel sad or cry or want the world to be different. Those are emotions and they come a step before the reactions that I am talking about. What I mean by your reaction is what you do next, after the emotion. Do you stare at The Body Shop and wonder if they are selling new taller, slimmer, stronger, whatever bodies? Do you go home and commit to a lifetime of exclusively shopping online? (I think that ship has sailed, anyway.) Or do you take that low moment and realise that it didn't break you, that you have just experienced something difficult and develop sympathy for yourself and maybe even for the people who made you feel so bad? Do you bounce back? Because if you do then you have controlled your reaction and you have grown stronger. I like to think of resilience being like a muscle, because muscles have to be tested, torn a little and regrown to become stronger. So don't hide from your emotions or suppress your natural reactions to the adversity of life – experience them, understand them and grow.

That is hard when you are young and even harder when people are not just making you feel different through their own carelessness but through their own effort, when they are actually trying to make you feel bad. My experience was that people only really started doing that once they became teenagers. At primary school, kids sometimes acted in the way that we have talked about – confused or intrigued by difference – but there was less of the spitefulness that means you have to develop that muscle of resilience. There was less of the kind of cruelty that requires you to step away, believe in yourself and be fearless enough to share the problem with people who can help. That was the kind of bullying that I experienced in secondary school and it was only by seeing the weakness of my bullies and seeking strength through the help of my family, mentors and teachers that I could overcome it. So keep that in mind because no one has the right to make you feel less than them and that there will always be people you can tell and who can help.

I really benefited from counselling and having a mentor at secondary school – someone who would listen without judgement and be there with a perspective wider than my own. That is particularly true when you are young but also as an adult in your professional or social life. It is so easy to be caught up in the moment and the space in which we are living or working and think that the problems we face are all-consuming. That is why speaking with someone who is one step removed, outside of your group or team, can allow you to find solutions that you otherwise wouldn't see from your perspective within the difficult situation. That is what my mentor did for me. She was amazing, a few years older than me and blessed with a calmness and perspective on the challenges that I was facing as a kid of 14. Still, though, I didn't tell her everything. I do regret that but I try not to dwell on it because regret is an emotion that takes up energy I could be using elsewhere.

I didn't even tell her about the day when three boys from my year picked me up and put me in an industrial waste bin. Seriously. It was horrible. They grabbed me and dropped me into it, then slammed the lid shut. In that cold darkness, surrounded by the smells of yesterday's lunches, all I could think was that they saw me as trash. Rubbish. Something less than them that was only worthy of the bin. I felt such a deep, deep shame that I couldn't even share what had happened with my mentor. Of course, I can now see that I had nothing to be ashamed of, that the guilt and self-consciousness should have been all my bullies', but that is what happens to us in situations when we are bullied.

We start to believe that the person who is bringing us down knows something we don't, that there must be something about us that makes them want to act this way. It may just be for one small second or in one small way, but that thought is the start of a negative cycle and it is a mistake we all have to be conscious to avoid.

If someone wants to put me in a bin then there is something wrong with them, not me. It is not because I am small, or different, or somehow the type of person who gets bullied. It is a result of the bully's limitations, because they haven't developed the skill of empathy and most likely because they have been hurt by someone else and just want to pass that hurt along down the chain. That's a really common reason why people bully others. They perhaps have been treated badly by their parents or friends and they have had that same thought that there may be something wrong with them. They start to believe that their bully must know something they don't, that the bully is somehow right – that their dad or sister who picks on them is better than them because they do hurtful things. So to make themselves feel better, to join the class of the bully rather than the bullied, they find a new person to add into that hurtful food chain beneath them. Instead of realising that no one deserves to be a victim, they decide that their best bet is to make sure they are at least one of the bullies instead. In their mind, if being bullied makes them feel wrong, being the bully is surely the way to be right.

That is why I think taking control of our reactions and rising above is such a powerful thing. This is how we can stop those reverberations of cruelty from continuing down the line, from my bully's bully down to them, on to me and then from me to someone else. When we rise above, the hate doesn't sink down towards the next victim, the next generation, the next year group or sibling. This means that the power to rise above is about more than just you, more than freeing yourself from fear. It allows you to create a release valve that lets a little bit of the cruelty in this world disappear. When you break the chain and rise above, that hurt which may have started years ago and travelled from person to person down the chain evaporates – and with that, you have changed the world.

That is what I mean by rising above being a strength, a sword in its own right rather than just a shield, because with it you can be a window through which the pain that has always bounced from one person to the next in our society can disappear. By not bottling it up and not passing it along, you not only become a stronger individual, you become a force for good. It helps me to know that when I block out the haters and rise above hate, I'm not just being neutral, I'm changing the world. So I hope you can remember this. People can sense that strength – a couple of the boys who put me in that bin have reached out to me on social media too recently to tell me how well I have done. Needless to say, I haven't tried to convince them of the errors in their past because that chain has been broken and I don't need them to feel worse to make myself feel better.

People ask me if I receive a lot of hate online and the answer is, not as much as you might expect. When I was first starting out, people would pipe up and say cruel things, but as time has gone on and my profile has grown, there have been a few changes. First, my fans have got my back. Anyone who wants to spray their unpleasantness my way gets met with a gang of my followers (Timboans? Fatimaniacs? Fatnatics?) who are more than ready to tell them what we stand for. We believe in mutual respect, love and laughter – so if you want to creep up like some digital skunk and leave your stench on my page then don't worry, we've got the Febreze (brand partnership pending).

Or you'll get blocked. Discovering that button was the second change in my relationship with online abuse. It is just a wonderful piece of technology. Bing. Block. Ding. Deleted. Just because I'm visible doesn't mean I have to listen to you, and just because I block you doesn't mean I can't take whatever it is you are serving, I've just got too many dishes on the menu, darling. I really can't recommend blocking enough. Try it some time, it's like the yin to the yang of swiping right on Tinder – Trollder you could call it – but instead of making someone turn up in your DMs and start two days of conversation that never leads to a date, it simply returns a troll to their cave with a beautiful efficiency.

Bullying, online or in the real world, is a serious issue and I don't think there is enough support for people of any age who are confronted with other people's hate. Counselling gave me the tools I'm sharing with you here to see other people's abuse as their problem not mine. It was a way to release the pressure valve in the presence of someone who could see my life without the blinkers that come from having to live within it. I'd like to see more counselling and therapy offered in schools, but, from what I can see, those services have only been reduced in the last few years. Child and adolescent mental health services in the UK have had their budgets slashed, schools and teachers are just trying to get their year groups through to exams and no one has the time or money to talk about how not to live miserably. If I had my way (Fats4PM 2025 – dw we got this), mental health support would be given to every teenager, training a new generation of counsellors would be a government priority and every workplace would have anonymous mental health and anti-bullying support available as standard. People should be able to talk. If you feel like your friend or boss is bullying you, it shouldn't be something that has to go to a workplace tribunal; it should be calmly discussed and acted upon in the way that you need to make you feel able to do your job.

So, in short, don't let the haters drag you down. Feel the emotions that come from their hurtful treatment but then understand their behaviour for what it is – a reflection of other people's limitations. When you are able to see that, and can rise above the conflict and the hurt, you will gain a perspective that allows you to challenge the hate in the world and change it for the better. So seek help, be brave enough to admit that you can't do it alone and then step forward, stronger in the knowledge that you are making the world a less hateful place.

Don't spend your energy fighting the bullies, whether they are someone you call your friend or three immature boys in your year, save it for changing the world. Don't believe a word your haters say but understand the insecurities that are making them say those things. Don't sink to their level, rise above and look down towards them with feelings of sympathy – because when you have risen from the experience of being bullied with your dignity intact and your perspective clear, you have grown. Your muscle of resilience has been strengthened and you will have gained the power to carry not only your own weight but that of the next person who is experiencing what you once went through.

The Timbo Takeaway

When others try to bring you down, don't hide from the hurt it causes. Be aware of your pain, be sympathetic to yourself and consider why that person has tried to hurt you. It is not because of any fault in you; it's a problem with them. Anyone who goes out of their way to make another person feel worse is only trying (and failing) to displace the pain that they feel. When you understand that and choose not to pass on the hurt that they have passed to you, you have broken a cycle and made the world a better place. That is what it means to rise above. You do not rise above your pain but above the natural urge to try to push it on to someone else.

Remember that no one has a right to bring you down. Understand the difference between challenging advice and hurtfulness. If someone you have cared about wants to hurt you, be fearless enough to challenge them and if they cannot change then be prepared to let them go. If they return and they have changed, be forgiving.

If someone you do not care about tries to hurt you, distance yourself from them. If they continue, seek help. No one can deal with a bully on their own but only we can stop ourselves from becoming bullies in response.

Be kind and expect kindness. See those who cannot give it as victims of a struggle that you won't join. Trust me, you will be more fearless for it.

Reflections

Think of a time someone was cruel to you. Now try to understand how they were trying to make themselves feel better by doing it. What sadness could they have been trying to unload on you?

Think of a time when you were cruel to someone else. Were you sad about something? What would you do differently and what would you say to that person now?

Who are the people you would tell if you had a problem with a bully? Practise saying the words to them so you know that it is something that you can do.

....
....
....
....
....
....
....
....
....
....
....

YOU HAVE TO KNOW THAT ANYONE WHO BRINGS YOU DOWN IS NOT WORTHY OF BEING CALLED YOUR FRIEND.

FRIENDSHIPS ARE PARTNERSHIPS THAT MAKE YOU BOTH STRONGER.

COMMANDMENT 4:

Trust the

Journey

The path to your dreams will at first seem so long, but if you learn to love the journey then you will never get tired.

I talk quite a lot in this book about following your dreams, about having goals and pursuing them fearlessly even when the world seems like it wants to block your path. Knowing where you are going and retaining your hope in the future is often the difference between giving up and carrying on. It certainly was for me. But as important as that is, I also want to talk about appreciating the present moment and making sure we don't wish it away while we look forward to better times.

We all have times where we wish that we could fast-forward life. Maybe it's your exam year, or the middle of a difficult project; maybe it's the night before a big show or match. You just wish you could be at the other end, with the achievement secured and all the stress and striving done. Now think back on those times with hindsight, about your GCSE year or the rehearsals for that show. If you are like me, you probably think that they were some of the best times in your life because those moments where you are striving and uncertain are what life is all about. Understanding that is really important because your achievements alone will never be enough to make you happy, whereas the process of achieving them and the good or bad times that come with it can be. If you can develop awareness that the path is as important as the destination, and that hard times will one day become fond memories, then you will never get tired of the journey and you will be revitalised and ready when your next one begins.

When I look back at my own struggles to get where I am now, I sometimes wish I could tell my former self to stop and enjoy the moment. Yes, there were moments when I was stressed, lonely or uncertain, but that's when I was really living. Without those times, life would just be one boring procession of easy and superficially satisfying experiences. So embrace the journey and the challenges that come with it and try to enjoy them. The truth is that there aren't really destinations in life, just different points where we put down markers and stop to look backward or forward – and even then we are still existing in the present. The present, the now, is all that there ever really is; your past was the present at some time and your future will be too, so learning to enjoy it is really an investment for your whole life.

Which is a long way of saying that there have been points when I doubted how my present could ever lead to the future I wanted, when I was too caught up in my plans to appreciate the moment I was in. So many times along the way, I have felt a tension between my belief in myself and the way life seemed to be going. For example, I knew I wanted to be a performer, that I wanted to make the world a place where disabled girls could be up there on the stage, but it just didn't feel like any of the stages I was approaching had space for me. That was how I was feeling when I dropped out of dance classes aged 11.

I had been dancing for six years at that point, but the little girl who had been rolling around the stage as a contortionist cat started to fall out of love with what she was doing. I never felt like I really belonged with my dance troupe, never made any real friends and I found that more and more, I was being passed over for good roles. Whenever we had a new show coming up and I tried for a big part, it felt like they thought I was too small. I don't need to tell you how that made me feel (clue: *not big*). So I packed it in. I made a choice that I don't recommend at any point in this book. I gave up and I missed out on the happiness that I could have felt because in the moment it didn't seem like it was going anywhere. I still kept dancing though – ain't no director gonna to steal my boogie. (Title for a disco track maybe? Song three on the album, after 'Love Is Your Superpower' and 'It's a Hard Block Life/Hater Riddim'.) In the school playground, all I needed was a clap or a beatbox and I was off again. My friends would crowd round and watch, and I'd go at it all break time. I didn't need anyone else with me and I didn't stop to think what the rest of the playground thought was going on, I just one, two-stepped it.

That was really my only creative outlet at that time. I wasn't making any videos or doing comedy, I was just trying to get through school and dance in a way that made me and other people smile. I wish I had found more ways to be creative as a teenager. In hindsight, I should probably have taken drama (because what is life but *drama*?). My only artistic outlet in secondary school was media studies. That had good and bad aspects. I learned a lot of the skills that I have put to use as a content creator, about shooting and editing videos, about bringing people together to make an attractive scene, but I also learned that I would probably have to do my own casting . . .

You see, in media studies, I faced the same problems that I did in my dance group. No one saw a little girl as a serious lead and that could hurt. Once, we were working on a short film project for GCSE. Everyone put themselves forward for on-screen roles but when it came to me, I didn't do myself justice. I said that maybe people wouldn't take it seriously if I was in it, that somehow I'd make the whole thing look silly just by being there. You can probably tell my self-esteem was low. In my mind, little people only appeared on camera as a comedy turn, the butt of the joke or a funny sidekick. I suggested that maybe for that reason it was best that I stay behind the scenes. The teacher agreed. For all that I wanted him to tell me differently – that there was nothing inherently silly about me and that my presence didn't turn the whole thing into a joke – he didn't. He suggested I was probably right and that maybe I should just focus on the editing. That hurt, but most of all, it hurts to look back at that girl and know she wasn't doing herself justice. I hope the world is a different place ten years down the line, that the increased visibility of disabled people has made teenagers like me look at themselves differently, but back then, I just felt I should stay in the shadows, even though something inside me craved the limelight. I can see now with the benefit of hindsight how that moment actually lit a fire in me. It showed me how other people's prejudices would hold me back if I let them and it drove me to make it so that no other girl has to experience a moment like I did.

Still, I learned useful lessons being behind the camera and, in many ways, it was a better use of my time than being centre stage. I don't need any help learning how to be the lead *dahhhhling*, but I did need to know about the craft of making a lead look good. I must have banked that knowledge because for a few years I didn't make any videos of my own. My social media at the time was really just Snapchat between friends; I had no plans to try to make anything public or entertaining. So I continued on my journey, I focused on my studies and worked hard (although I'm *still* waiting on my African Daughter of the Year 2014 award). It meant that I did well in my exams and continued on to college. Which was also often hard.

While I was there, I didn't have many friends. I had decided to study at a sixth-form college outside of my area to expand my horizons, but I realise now that I wasn't yet in a place where I had the self-confidence to branch out and I was still allowing my past experiences to constrain my present. I still needed people to approach me before I would start to build a relationship with them. That was a legacy of being poorly treated, othered and bullied, and it meant that I could only really connect with people who made a big effort to try to connect with me. That is a *very* small pool when you are dealing with other self-conscious 16-year-olds who probably haven't met someone who looks like you before.

I did meet one amazing boy, though – Osmond, who had the confidence and maturity to reach out. We were both working in a library closer to my home and he came up to me and started a conversation. He recognised me from college and went out of his way to make a connection. We were friends for the next two years, hanging out and studying together, and it made that difficult time feel better. I see now that it was much more than that and I wish I had been more focused on the moment so I could have seen how special it was to have that time with him. Osmond passed away last year and I hope that if his family are reading this, you know that he was a light in my life, someone who made me feel valuable when I thought others were ignoring me, a one in a million soul. My friendship with Osmond is an example of what I mean when I talk about not wishing away the difficult times. If you'd told me then that I was going to be a performer in a few years, surrounded by amazing people, and offered me the chance to fast-forward my life, I would have taken it. But then I would never have had that time with him. Whereas now, I would do anything to go back there and study with him again. You never know what you have until it's lost, so don't wish time away.

My urge to perform still bubbled beneath the surface throughout college, and by the time I arrived at university, I had started to see people become successful as performers on the internet and thought that it could be a path for me. I had no clue how I was going to do it but I had an unshakeable belief that I could. Something in me said that there would be a chance and when it came I would have to take it. So I kept on working, studying hard for a degree in accounting that I didn't really want so that if my dreams never came true I had a back-up, and if they did, well, then I could count my money using the relevant software. In truth, it was a bit deeper than *just* learning to count money, but not much. I'm dyslexic so I found wordy subjects challenging at school, but I always flourished at maths. Written numbers somehow made sense in a way that written words didn't, so the combination of my family's expectations and my own desire to educate myself led me into a practical degree that built on my love of numbers.

I have to admit, though, that no amount of number love stopped me feeling like my chance of achieving my real dream was slipping away. With each passing day, there was a growing fear that my hopes of being a performer would never come true. This meant that even though I was young, healthy and surrounded by good people, I was never fully able to enjoy my life and trust the journey.

Then, one day at university, there was a moment that truly made my hopes rise. Something that caught my eye as I washed my hands in a leaky bathroom basin. It was a small thing. A piece of paper tacked on to a toilet door in a dingy corner of my university building. That hope which had beaten hard in my chest since the day I first hopped on a stage began to raise its tempo. I am not afraid to admit that I got an adrenaline surge from a ripped-up piece of A4. It was a casting call for a fashion project aimed at showcasing different body types, and in particular, disabled women. I can't describe to you how fast my fingers dialled the number on that page or how hard I tried to slow down my heart and calm my voice as an answer came down the line.

'Hello?' the voice said.

'Hi, I saw an advert for your inclusive casting here at my uni. It *might* be something I'd be interested in.' (All the while thinking, *THIS IS MY SHOT. INCLUDE ME. I AM INCLUSIVE AND SHOULD BE INCLUDED.*)

The woman on the line asked for my details and emailed me later that day. At home that evening, I lay in bed scrolling up and down the email, refreshing my inbox in case they had followed up to say they had made a mistake, and checking that I hadn't misread the invitation. I imagined all the possibilities of how I could have got it wrong. '*Oh sorry, we said "exclusive" casting call. You'll have to be excluded first.*' Or '*Nooooo, it's a* reclusive *casting call; you'll need to live in the woods if you want to get this job.*' Tbh I would probably have gone full lumberjack if they'd said that.

But I wasn't wrong. The wording was just as I had first seen it and they really did seem to be looking for women with disabilities for a modelling shoot. Now, I know you might be thinking that it's not so out of the ordinary, that we see a lot more disabled people in adverts and fashion these days. And you'd be right. Thanks to the hard work of good people, it's becoming less extraordinary. BUT IN A TOILET IN HENDON IN 2017 IT FELT VERY BLOOMIN' EXTRAORDINARY. Sorry I'm shouting but it felt like my fairy toilet godmother from north London had arrived and would you *please pass me those glass slippers*?

Though I was also sort of wrong. Well, at least, *I* wasn't. Everything else was. When I arrived at the call, I looked around the waiting area and saw at least 15 other girls with no visible disabilities, except for one girl who had alopecia. If this was an inclusive casting call it was including a few too many people, if you asked me. I tried not to let it get me down. I *couldn't* let it get me down. I had waited too long and I couldn't let my fear of my own difference shake my confidence.

When I went into the room with the scouts, though, I surprised even myself. I'm sure you've heard of faking it till you make it? Whatever you picture when you think of that then dial it up a few notches – because I faked so well I even started to believe myself. It went something like this:

Scout: Would you describe yourself as a confident person?

Fats: Of course. In fact, I'm so confident I may be the most confident person you've ever confided in.

Scout: Erm, OK. And how would you feel about being in an underwear campaign; do you mind showing off your body?

Fats [INTERNAL DIALOGUE]: YES I MIND SHOWING OFF MY BODY A BIT IF I'M HONEST. I'VE STILL GOT SOME HANG-UPS.

Fats [EXTERNAL DIALOGUE]: No! I love my body and I think the world needs to see it.

Scout: So you'd be happy for your family to see a billboard of you in your underwear out in public?

Fats [INTERNAL]: NO!!

Fats [EXTERNAL]: Of course!

The truth is, I *could* be happy for my family to see me like that, and I *could* be comfortable showing off my body . . . just after a bit of processing time. I absolutely was not ready to do it at that moment, but with a bit of a chance to think about it, to consider what it could do for representation and, *ahem,* me, I was fully down. In that moment, I was just ready to grasp that chance and I was answering each question in the affirmative *Yes Sir/Madam!*

Looking back, I'm impressed by that girl. Only I know how awkward and different she still felt, that she'd never really been made to feel beautiful, and yet she still went out there and shot her shot. Props to you 2017 Fats, we couldn't have done it without you – your main character energy was enough to make a main character out of me.

I did three shoots and even before I had seen the pictures, I felt a real confidence boost. It was almost like the person I had told myself to be in the casting came to life once I did the shoot, as if seeing others accept that projection of a more confident Fats made me believe that she really did exist. It was a useful life lesson that I've held on to ever since. If I aim for goals that exceed my grasp, try to do things which at first I think I can't, the process of reaching for them always leads to some growth. After I left the final shoot, I just thought, *Wow! If I've done that I can do anything.*

The campaign dropped according to plan and I thought it might be the start of a long-awaited modelling career. I'd tried to join an agency for diverse models as a teenager, but all they had done was take my money and tell me no one was looking for little people. Now, I was in an underwear campaign.

When the pictures arrived I put them on my Instagram. At this point, my social media profiles were pretty ordinary. I was only followed by family and friends and couldn't really see a path from there to a more public profile, but when the first picture from that campaign dropped, people started following from everywhere. It was like I could feel the ground moving beneath my feet, a mountain of potential rising up beneath me as the tectonic plates of my growing self-belief and a receptive world pressed up against one another. More and more people began to follow the page and messages of appreciation and support came flooding in. I think what happened was that, without knowing it, I had touched a nerve. Underwear campaigns are a sensitive subject for a lot of people, a place where society's body images get defined and a lot of people feel alienated. This was an inclusive campaign that showcased disabled people, as well as colour palettes designed for darker-skinned women, and that really seemed to break through. My willingness to be vulnerable, to put myself forward for that job and to be seen seemed to make a lot of other people feel seen too. At the time, I thought I had just applied for a job, but looking back now, I see that it was actually an act of defiance: I was rebelling simply by being unashamed of myself.

At that moment, I committed to riding the wave of attention my social media account was getting and rising on that mountain. I sensed the momentum building and I knew that this was what I had been preparing for, what I had always tried to manifest.[1] I had tried to think carefully about what I wanted, how I would pursue it when the time came and kept believing that it would happen. So I followed my plan and my instincts. I approached my social media channels professionally, posting regularly and with a clear focus on creating a high standard of content. It made sense because I wanted it to be my profession, and also because I was trusting in the process and therefore the journey. If you have a clear process – rules that you follow and

---

1   Some people say that manifesting has these amazing, supernatural powers. That's not what I believe. I just think that the process of picturing yourself positively in the place you want to be can encourage optimism, preparation for opportunities and belief in your methods when those opportunities arise – and those are powerful things, with real impacts.

positive steps that you reliably take – then you can have full faith in the journey you are on.

Side note: if you are trying to establish yourself or your work through an online platform like social media then I would recommend a few things. First, do approach posting like a professional. Your personal accounts can be the place where you put up silly sideways shots from the cab on the way back from a night out, because that's fun, but your work channels (and they are actually work, not social) should be approached with planning and careful consideration. The second idea, which follows from the first, is to be consistent. Post at similar times each day in a routine that your followers can get used to; it helps to think of your channel like a TV station or radio show that people like to tune into regularly. Third, think about creating high-quality content, not likes or getting people to like you. We want our friends to like us but in the professional world, we should aim to be respected. I think the fact that they're called 'social' channels gives people a misconception about them – sure, they can be used for socialising, but in a professional sense, they are more like publicity tools, entertainment channels or news/ information services. So if you want to make a career for yourself working with social media then try to approach it as if you are a PR person, an entertainment professional or a journalist. That has the added benefits of encouraging a high standard of work as well as a healthy distance from the people on there who want to make you feel low. You can show your personality but never confuse your online persona with your *self*.

So back to it. A few months after adopting a more professional approach to social media, I was approached for my first TV job, which was good news. It was for the Channel 4 series *The Undateables*. Which was . . . *news*. I didn't know whether to laugh or cry. I had still not had a serious relationship at that point and the last thing I wanted to be told was that I was undateable on national television. Equally, it wasn't really a professional job as people on *The Undateables* aren't necessarily performers. I wanted to be seen as a professional (and a *dateable* professional at that) and I'm not sure I had the confidence in myself or my public profile to take the job at that time, so I turned it down.

A few months passed and I thought more about the show. It was clear that they had seen something in me and the more I thought about the opportunity, the more I saw it as another situation of faking it till you make it. Just because the show was called *The Undateabless*, it didn't necessarily mean I was, and if I wanted to build a profile for myself then I needed to be willing to go into uncharted territory with my head held high. So I phoned the producer and before I knew it, a camera crew was in my front room.

I wasn't used to that. It was a strange experience but I knew it was a part of the steep learning curve that I was on. I had my doubts, for sure. I worried about how it would turn out, whether people would judge me or only see me as the girl from *The Undateables*, but each time the doubts arose in my mind, I reassured myself that this was the path that I had chosen and that if I was going to be in the public eye I would have to get used to other people's opinions. I think the process of turning your private life into a public one is a challenge for anyone who achieves a degree of recognition, but it was probably easier for me – I was already used to people staring, strangers asking oddly personal questions about my health or body, and I knew what it was like for people to make assumptions about me before we had even met. So I guess you could say I was prepared for a life of recognition.

Looking back over that uncertain period of my life, where I didn't have any idea of how I could pursue creativity, I feel sympathy for the girl I was. It is hard to feel positive in moments of uncertainty, to remain present and appreciative when you are still striving, but remembering some stories from my late teens and early twenties reminds me that those times were a blessing. I met some wonderful people and I had time to develop skills and discover who I wanted to be. Maybe if my goals had been achieved sooner, I wouldn't have had the time to develop the maturity to process them or the mental resilience to adapt. Mainly, though, thinking back to that time reminds me to enjoy the moment I am in even when there is uncertainty. My past, which felt so challenging when it was the present, is something I would love to experience again. I would love to have a day with people like Osmond who are no longer here. I would tell myself that there is never a good reason to wish you could fast-forward your life because someday you will be more than happy to rewind.

So enjoy the journey. You'll look back on it fondly when you reach your destination and you'll get there with a smile on your face if you do.

The Timbo Takeaway

Don't miss the joy in your present because of your investment in the future. Taking pleasure in the moment is no impediment to your success – in fact, it is a key component of it. Life is made up of moments, a series of presents that soon become the past and roll forward to become what you once called the future. So if you develop the skill of enjoying the moment you are in, you will be able to look back on your past fondly and enjoy your future deeply.

I know it can be hard. I know that the challenges you face day to day as you strive for your dreams can be frightening and that sometimes you would take the chance to skip to the moment you had 'made it' if you could. But you must remember that you have made it already. You are already the main character of your own life. You are alive and that is a special thing. So to be living, to be struggling for something is a blessing and the struggle is 90 per cent of the fun.

Finally, know that if you have accomplished

everything, if you have 'made it', then there is nothing left to make and no one wants that. So enjoy the process and love the journey because then you'll never get tired. Be fearless, be present and enjoy both the easy and the hard times. Then you will have done more than made it. You will have lived it.

Reflections

Has there been a time in your life when you wished days away? A Monday where you would have loved to skip forward to Friday? A challenging period you just wanted to press fast-forward? Now imagine looking back on that time as an elderly person. Think about how small the challenges might seem from a distance and how much joy it would give you to spend time back with those people and in that place.

Think about a really happy time in your life. Was that really a moment when you had nothing to worry about? Or are you just remembering the good things? Try to imagine right now as one of those happy times – what are the things you might appreciate and the worries that you might forget once this time has passed?

Write down five things that worried you in the past but that don't scare you now.

1. ....

2. ....

3. ....

4. ....

5. ....

Now write down five things that worry you now, which might seem small in the future.

1. ....
2. ....
3. ....
4. ....
5. ....

And finally, try writing down three things that you are grateful for *today*. If you can, do it again tomorrow and the next day, and onwards. You will find that there is a lot.

1. ....
2. ....
3. ....

THE PRESENT, THE NOW, IS ALL THAT THERE EVER REALLY IS; YOUR PAST WAS THE PRESENT AT SOME TIME AND YOUR FUTURE WILL BE TOO...

SO LEARNING TO
ENJOY IT IS REALLY
AN INVESTMENT FOR
YOUR WHOLE LIFE.

COMMANDMENT 5:

Only Doubt

Doubt Itself

**The words
'I can't' only
become true if
'you don't'.**

We left each other at the end of the last chapter with my life in a good place. It must have seemed like my fairy tale was set to have a happy ending. I'd modelled (tick), got a TV job (tick) and decided that online entertainment could provide me with a platform to spread my message and develop my career. The end. Our book's main character, Princess Fatima, lived happily ever after. Right? Wrong, because there was a wake-up call coming my way and that princess was about to go to sleep for a long time. There was no sign of a handsome prince coming my way, not even a frog or a magic bean, because when university finished, the big, bad expanse of adult life opened up in front of me and it was a lot.

Have you ever been in that position? When the safety net of formal education gets removed, after a lifetime of knowing what you are doing and where you are heading, you face real uncertainty for the first time. It is the moment when standing on your own two feet becomes real, the ground gets slippery and the wind picks up. Bills. Job searches. Conversations with proud aunties about their sons and daughters who all seem to be doctors/lawyers/ heads of the Sierra Leonean space programme. At that point, pursuing your dreams can feel even harder, as you simultaneously need them to come true more than ever but also have to support yourself financially while you work towards them. You have to earn money in the present while also working for free in the name of a future that you hope someday will pay the bills. If you find yourself in that place, you have to stay strong, stay focused and keep doubt at bay. You need to be fearless.

The specific struggles I had after university might have been a feature of my life and a result of my choices, but, even so, I believe that the lessons I learned can be applied more broadly. All of us stand at a crossroads at some point in our lives and likely experience the fear and doubt of trying to decide on the best path. I want to tell you how I overcame that doubt, about a time when self-belief and dedication were all that I had and – eventually – all that I needed.

I finished my accountancy course at university

and for a time, everything seemed rosy. I travelled for a while and my horizons seemed broad and my possibilities endless. When I came home, I celebrated graduation with my family and it was incredible to see their pride at my first-class honours degree. Not bad for a girl with dyslexia who had always seemed more interested in the looks than the books. I was chuffed but as we settled down to a celebratory dinner, the first plates had hardly hit the table before I heard those magic words, 'So, Fatima, have you decided what you are going to do next?'

My stomach dropped.

Thanks, guys. You didn't even give me a night to enjoy it. I had spent 20 years on the road to becoming a degree holder and I got a sum total of about four hours before I was asked to choose my next route. There was no time to bask in any glory, to celebrate reaching my destination. I'm sure you can understand now why I feel so strongly about enjoying the journey – because before you have even realised one is done, someone will start you on another one. You may be the main character in your life but spend enough time with your family and they'll always find a side quest for you.

I knew the answer that my parents wanted to hear. They wanted me to put my accountancy degree to some use. I had racked up plenty of debt to gain a qualification that would get me a job and the obvious response was to get a job that dealt with that debt. I needed to be an accountant. I didn't *want* to be an accountant but I knew that my honest answer to the question of 'what next?' wouldn't really cut it. I mean, what could I say?

'Oh, don't worry, Dad, I'm gonna work on this thing called TikTok.'

'What's that?'

'Well, it's a bit like Instagram.'

'And what's that?'

'It's a bit like Facebook.'

'What's . . .'

'Don't worry. I'll find a job.'

Because in my parents' eyes, social media was just pictures and talking. Not work. Not a career. I might as well have told them I was going to be a professional WhatsApper or a text-message artist. They didn't have a darned clue about social media and even if they did, the only way I was going to convince them that it counted as a job was if it paid.

Looking back, they were right. As always. The simplest definition of a job is something you get paid to do and at that time, I was not getting paid for being on socials. I was more like . . . a *volunteer*. So until being a social media creative paid my bills it was a hobby, an outlet, but certainly not a career. At best, it was the foundation upon which a job could be made – but until that foundation started carrying some serious weight, I had to do something a little more conventional.

So what do you think the diligent daughter with the accounting degree told her two NHS-employed parents she would do?

You guessed it. She told them she'd be an accountant for the NHS. For a bit. Only for a little bit. Until my real work took off. So I signed up with an agency and they got me a place in no time. Within a week, I was working in a hospital and ensuring that the ins and outs all added up – from the syringes to the wheelchairs, from doctors' salaries to toilet paper, I had to make sure that nothing was being missed and all was being accounted for. If you ever want to get an idea of how complicated a system like the NHS is, how brilliant and complex and time-consuming the whole thing has to be, look at the accounts. Keeping you and me healthy takes a lot of planning, and a lot of budgets, and I was a small cog in the big machine that ensured those budgets all got spent according to plan. I enjoyed being able to see behind the scenes of the system in which my parents worked, where my life had been saved and improved at so many points, but I admit that I could only do so because I saw it as temporary. It was a glorified summer job for me, something to pass the time as my real career grew.

But then it didn't.

Months went by and when those months became almost a year it felt like time to think about the day job more seriously. So I took a better paid position in the accounts department of a housing company. For some reason, it felt hard to do, like making that step somehow solidified my position as an accountant and made my other career less likely, but I overcame the doubt. My dream career had to come true and it was no good working in less well-paid jobs because they felt more temporary. I had to just *know* that anything else was temporary and keep my head up.

But try telling that to me on one of those Monday mornings when I trudged into work, though. I was filling spreadsheets for a company that I didn't care about, with people who didn't treat me well, in a job that I didn't enjoy, and it felt like it would last forever. It took every ounce of strength that I had to believe that it wouldn't break me before I got my shot. Of course, I don't think there is anything wrong with working in accounts and I don't want you to think that I am demeaning anyone who does. I studied accounting; I know that without accountants the world would probably fall apart. But it wasn't for me. If you work in accounts and you like your job, or it allows you to do the things you want to do in life, then more power to you sister/brother – you account like there is no tomorrow. My problem was that the work was doing precisely the opposite for me – it was stopping me from doing the things that I wanted to do and it was draining away my soul. I kid you not, if my life was a video game then you would see the Fats character with a little green bar marked 'soul' beneath her avatar. From Monday to Friday, you would watch it steadily slip from full towards just above zero and a warning sign would appear – *'soul levels critical'* – before my character would wobble to some weekend checkpoint where a DJ would play enough James Brown to keep me from becoming one of the undead. I was very unhappy but I knew that I couldn't let my disappointment at where I was lead me to doubt where I could get to. Unfortunately, that is often what happens – our unhappiness in the present leads us to become pessimistic about the future, making us more likely to get stuck.

I knew I was on a track that I desperately wanted to get off and, although my Instagram had stalled and no more modelling jobs were coming, I decided that I couldn't give up. As much as I sometimes lost faith that things could ever change, I had to keep believing that they would. Or I wouldn't have the energy to make the changes I needed to make. So I decided to work harder. To work smarter and better. But *not* in my day job at the accounts department. Oh *no hunny*, I fully phoned that job in eight hours a day to save my energy for the sorts of things a main character would do, things that would get me out of that place. I worked weekends in a club and spent my evenings making content because they were the things that gave me hope and meaning.

I think that meaning is an important word in this conversation. Any job can give you meaning if it allows you to do the things that you love in life. Whether that is having a family, snowboarding or rehoming wild chinchillas that have been caught up in the fur trade (if by some chance you are the person who does all three of those, hit me up as I think we can draft a pilot for a show together. *Fats and Snowboard Mum save the world with an army of rehabilitated chinchillas by their side* ★guitar riff). Even better, though, is if your job itself is something that provides you with meaning. Maybe the snow-chinchilla rescue corporation is hiring, so my advice is to know what is significant to you and to think practically about how you can build a career with it. Most of all, though, never doubt that you can make it, because the hardest moments in my life at that point were not the Monday mornings but the minutes when I let doubt creep into my mind.

The best moments, on the other hand, all came during my weekend job. I was a dancer in an exotic cabaret. Yes, friend, you heard me right. *Exotic cabaret* (that always sounds better in a sort of Nigella Lawson voice). No, I wasn't stripping and yes, I had to convince my parents that I was *definitely not stripping*. It was a hard sell at first. They worried that I had taken the logical step from clothed student to underwear model to nude dancer, but I was able to show them that this was a dancing job and I *needed it*. I needed it in my present and I needed it for my future, because from the day I finished university to the one where I started working at the club, everything had seemed to go downhill. The job at the cabaret reminded me of what I was going to do, of the world outside my office's four walls and the different ways in which I could perform and create.

It helped that the club, Cirque Le Soir, is absolutely *SLAMMIN'*. It's like a fever dream, or maybe a crazy, sexy nightmare that you don't really want to leave. It's a magical place, filled with strongmen and snake charmers, little people and giants, hot people and ice-cool celebs. People go there to have a more interactive night out. No sticky floors and alcopops, just class, a sense of magic and a touch of danger. Which is perfect for me. I love things which seem somehow otherworldly, like magic shows or high-wire acts which make you feel like the boundaries of possibility are stretching in front of your eyes. They remind you that our world is magical in so many ways and that we only convince ourselves it is all very ordinary to keep things manageable. At the club, I wore super-cool outfits, was part of group dance performances, supported other acts when they were on stage and was generally just a part of the vibe. It was not an ordinary job and I felt extraordinary doing it, which really gave me a boost and built my self-esteem.

People probably imagine it is quite high intensity

and high stress working as a performer in a place like Cirque Le Soir. The combination of alcohol and acrobats could make you think that but actually, it was really relaxed from a performer's perspective. It didn't feel like work, it felt like being part of a troupe. I was part of a gang of little people who I loved. They were mostly older than me and all had such powerful perspectives. They had faced the identity challenges that I had and every last one of them had discovered strength in the face of a world that wanted to undermine their difference. They made me proud to be unique.

I also met some really cool celebrities. Everyone from Ludacris to Jamie Foxx and French Montana came in when they were in London filming or doing shows and they were all lovely. One celeb, a musician (that I won't name), once gave me the job of finding the woman in the club who had the biggest booty. Just like that, he asked straight up – *excuse me, can you find the woman here with the biggest booty?* I said absolutely and set about my job diligently. I rushed around the club, my eyes well placed at about booty level, taking into consideration a number of booty factors. Size, depth, height, weight, shape. I was a business-like, equal opportunities booty evaluator but I did feel like I hadn't been given enough information. 'Biggest' can mean so many things. Is it relative booty? Absolute booty? Widest? Weightiest? I learned a lot about my booty principles that night. In the end, I took my job so seriously, developing a longlist which I whittled down to a shortlist before deciding on Miss Booty 2019, that when I arrived back at said rapper's table, he had left. Ah well, I thought, not a bad night's work.

I'm probably a really bad feminist in some people's eyes for being involved in that. Maybe I was also being a bad disability advocate by being part of the show. Sometimes, I just have to go on feeling and in these two cases I didn't think the attention was negative. Big booties were left out of the picture of human beauty standards for a long time, just like people with dwarfism were often left out of the entertainment industry. So if I come across cases where there are opportunities for big bums and little people to have a moment in the sun, and if those opportunities seem to come from a positive place, then I'll go more with my intuition than any theory. (I can't believe I have just explained my view of disability representation through a midnight butt search.)

Another night, I met Jamie Foxx at the club

and of all the celebrities I met, he was particularly swoontastic and sweet. I don't really vibe with arrogance and humility is a beautiful thing in talented people, but I would have forgiven Jamie Foxx for being at least a little bit up himself. He can sing, dance, act, do impressions and be generally gorgeous and yet he *still* manages to be humble. On the night that he was in he treated all of us performers as his equals, as fellow entertainers. That was an amazing thing.

Meeting those artists really helped me. They seemed so normal, just people who had pursued their passion and taken opportunities when they arose. They didn't have some supernatural glow, or a laser-like focus which marked them out from everyone else, and it reminded me that I didn't need to change myself to pursue my dreams; I just had to be resilient. So I resolved to do just that and I planned my escape route from the nine-to-five. I would get management for my social media work and try to start getting some income from it. I would make videos regularly and professionally, and I would set a date for when I would be out of office for life. Six months, I said. That was my plan. Six months and I would support myself with my own creations.

I find that planning is a powerful antidote to doubt. Often, our anxiety is a fear of the unknown, so the creation of a plan, a timetable or a road map can give you some 'knowables' to turn to when the uncertainty gets too much. If, like me, you have decided on your goals but get caught up sometimes in the fear that they won't or can't come true, then try visualising the steps it will take you to get where you want to be. Start by thinking about the goal and gradually take steps back from it until you arrive at the beginning – which is where you are now. When you have that plan, you will be able to see that your dream is a very real thing, which will be realised by following clear steps. Those steps will be manageable, doable things that together lead you to something that you may have once thought too big to achieve. The steps and the plan give you something real, something certain, during a time when uncertainty itself is the most frightening thing. So trust me, a plan will help.

Unless, of course, the world goes into lockdown due to an unforeseeable global pandemic. That may be a hard one to factor into your plans.

You guessed it. I started my six-month plan for getting out of office life just as Covid-19 hit. While that certainly took me out of the office (hello, home working), the onset of a pandemic didn't necessarily feel like an opportunity for me to progress in my career as a creator. Now I was just an office worker without an office and a dancer without a club. But I did have my one other creative outlet available to me: I was still able to make content. And whereas before, my creative time was limited to evenings and some parts of the weekends, now I was able to think about filming videos during my lunch break, to get down to editing as soon as I clocked off and to use a bit of my locked-down life to pay more attention to what was proving popular online. That was a game changer. By watching others who were doing well and tracking the progress different people made by focusing on certain trends, I was able to see that you could have much more success if you knew what was going on around you online.

My decisions to be professional about posting and to respond positively to other people doing well were key in allowing me to take my opportunities when they came. When we are experiencing self-doubt, the success of others can feel like a problem, as if their achievements take up room that we would otherwise have been able to step into ourselves. For me, though, having the self-belief to see the success of others as encouragement and a template for my own success meant that I was able to learn. If I had doubted myself or been bitter about how well other people were growing their social media accounts, I would have missed the opportunity to learn from them and, later, to collaborate with them. Remembering that there is enough success to go around is a key philosophy in my life. Someone else doing well is better thought of as an opportunity than a problem for you.

I joined TikTok. I watched people who were making progress on the platform and I resolved to take similar approaches to them – their schedules, their ability to jump on trends and to learn from those moments when they made mistakes. As I said in the last chapter, it helps to approach your social channels as a professional rather than an individual and although my content has always been true to my life and my experiences, the ways in which I have packaged it and presented it have always been open to development based on what I have seen others doing well. So I followed, and I thought, and I posted. On repeat. I continued to phone in my work with the accounts team (literally by this point) but in my spare moments, I took notes on successful TikTokers, trends that seemed to be catching people's attention and video styles that would fit well with my creativity.

Steadily, my following started to grow. People from my Instagram began moving over to follow me on TikTok and new fans started to emerge. At times, I compared myself to other people on the channel who were further along than me, which can be positive or negative. I tried to keep it positive by comparing the quality of our content rather than quantity of followers, because I believed that if I maintained the first then the second would come. When it comes to making comparisons between us and other people on social media, it's really important to be positive and productive. A lot of people end up with negative self-esteem and self-doubt because they compare themselves to other people on social media in damaging ways. We tell ourselves we are less beautiful than them, less fortunate or less talented, and that can really magnify the self-doubt into an even bigger problem. My advice is to try to see those other people in a positive light; treat them as examples or case studies to learn from rather than sources of doubt. Know that you are valuable and interesting, and that someone else being valued or the subject of interest doesn't change that. Compare yourself in so far as it drives you to do the things you love better but don't let comparison make you love yourself less.

The six-month period that I had marked out for my professional transition slipped away quickly – though, as I think we can all agree, time moved strangely in lockdown. Steadily, though, I found myself feeling more confident that I could meet my targets in the long term. I got my first manager for social media opportunities and an opportunity to go on BBC Radio London to speak to the amazing Eddie Nestor.[2] I really began to see how I could make it as a creative and a spokesperson for disabled people. But, then again, I had believed all along that I could do it, which is what made it possible.

So there was no fairy-tale ending. It wasn't a handsome prince or some dubious trade in magical beans that helped me move towards a place where I wanted to be, but hard work and self-belief. The hard work was essential for making progress and the self-belief stopped me from falling apart at times when that progress stalled. There were so many points at which I could have lost hope, questioned

---

2 Shout-out to Eddie. He is an amazing broadcaster and an even more amazing person who has believed in me from day one.

my abilities or doubted whether the world would really want to hear from someone like me. My whole life I had been stared at, othered and told I was different, and it was only my self-belief that allowed me to turn that into a strength rather than a fear. My bullies and my dance and media teachers had done nothing to make me believe in myself, but the truth is that is why it is called self-belief – it has to come from you. That can be particularly hard to develop if you live in the social media age and make your career online. So much of your success is tied to people's immediate responses to you, but I want you to remember that those responses cannot change how *you* look at you. At the end of the day, the only way to be fearless is to have true belief in yourself, that you are enough and you have enough time, and then to separate that belief from the way that other people respond to you. So do not get too high when the world seems to love you and do not get low when hate comes your way. Be constant, doubtless and fearless because then you will be able to do anything. And if you know what it is you want to do, you will be unstoppable.

The Timbo Takeaway

We all doubt ourselves sometimes, particularly during periods of our lives when things aren't going our way. Remember, though, that these are the times when our self-belief is tested and when it is most valuable. Because the only way that we change a situation we are unhappy with is by believing that we can and creating a plan for how we will. So decide what you want and where you want to be, create a plan composed of small steps and manageable milestones, and then work towards them one at a time.

Remember that other people won't always be able to understand your dream; they may not know enough about your world or the world in which your dream exists may simply not have been made yet. So don't be afraid to make it and don't let other people's expectations define what you think is possible. Work with others, those who you trust and whose opinions you value, but remember, at the end of the day, you have to believe and trust in yourself first and foremost.

Be careful when you make comparisons. A comparison can be useful if it provides lessons, if you can learn from what someone else is doing or how they are doing it, but if you are comparing yourself aimlessly or negatively, then stop. Comparing yourself to another person and feeling worse about yourself does no good, but using it as a means to see how you can be better, by your own standards, is useful. A lot of us find social media makes us think about what we are not, what we can't do or what we lack, and we have to stay strong to avoid that. Remind yourself of who you are, what you love about yourself and what you have, and then if you want to be comparative, think about the ways in which you can learn from someone else about how to show it publicly.

You are valuable and you should never doubt it because the only thing to doubt is doubt itself. There are much better things to be spending your time and energy on. Finally, remember that the most frightening things are often the ones that lead us to grow – the challenges that make us work harder and reach higher – so be conscious of your fears and approach them fearlessly, because then you can show the world the person you know you are. The person that you believe in.

Reflections

Think of something that you were once scared to do but did. Now write down how that process made you feel. What were your thoughts before you did it, while you did it and what were your feelings once you had faced that challenge?

Now think of something that you are currently scared to do. What is it that makes you feel fear or doubt? Is it other people's opinions? Ask yourself how your own self-belief could help you overcome them. Is it failure? Ask yourself how bad that would really be. Ask yourself whether failure even really exists if you are able to try again. And then again. And again. Because you only really fail if you don't try or if you give up.

Think about someone who you compare yourself to in a way that makes you doubt yourself. Now, starting from a place of self-belief (it can be imagined . . . *for now*), consider the ways in which you can learn from them. How might that person make you try harder? What skills or approaches can you learn from them?

Think about what gives you meaning. What is it that you wake up and feel excited about? Could that be something that you build into your life?

Make a five-step plan for how you would do it. Remember: the goal can change and the path can too, but as long as you have something to work towards and ideas of how you will do it, life will feel meaningful and you will feel powerful.

1. ....
....
....

2. ....
....
....

3. ....
....
....

4. ....
....
....

5. ....
....
....

NEVER DOUBT THAT YOU CAN MAKE IT, BECAUSE THE HARDEST MOMENTS IN MY LIFE AT THAT POINT WERE NOT THE MONDAY MORNINGS ...

BUT THE MINUTES WHEN I LET DOUBT CREEP INTO MY MIND.

COMMANDMENT 6:

Discover New

Perspectives

If you have the chance to see the world, then do. You will see yourself differently when you discover new perspectives.

Perspective is the ability to see the world and our life from different angles, to discover the light and the shade that make up the picture and realise that nothing is fixed and nothing is given. In a good way. It allows us to see in more dimensions and to reach much deeper and more satisfying levels of understanding. With perspective, we can see how many things can be true all at once – how we can be both lucky and unlucky, how we are both enough and can always be better, how we are all different and in some ways we are all fundamentally the same.

When I have been struggling with the hand I've been dealt and asked 'Why me?', I've come to understand that the only answers that really do justice to such a difficult question are those that come from a shift in perspective: for example, 'Why not me?' or 'Why someone else instead?' It is easy to fixate on the unfairness of life when it smacks us in the face, but with perspective we can see that other people have their own pain. So if I am going to ask 'Why me?' when something is wrong at my end, I need to keep in mind that there have been a thousand things not going wrong for me and a thousand things going wrong for others in that same moment.

Seeing the world from other people's perspectives allows us to appreciate those things in our lives that we take for granted and sympathise with others on aspects of theirs that we might not even have considered. I'm not religious but I think that a sense of perspective – particularly about the challenges others face – is something that religion often helps people to develop. You see it in how most religions treat care for those living in poverty as a central belief. They ask their followers to think about those who have less than them, to understand their perspective, and I think that is as important now as it has ever been.

Maybe it is even more important? I spend my life on social media and I know better than anyone the good that it can do, the opportunities and connections that it creates, but I also know that it leads a lot of people to make comparisons based on a limited perspective. Many of us go on social media and look at people who seem to be more fortunate than ourselves – richer, funnier, more beautiful – and that is a problem and an issue of perspective in more ways than one.

Firstly, we cannot know what the lives of those people we envy are really like. Maybe they feel like they have created a myth and they do not feel as rich or funny or beautiful as they seem, and they feel trapped by the impression they create. We have all had that feeling of wishing we were always as beautiful as we appeared in *that photo,* with *that make-up,* on *that day,* but now imagine if you had convinced the world that *that photo* was the *real you.* Imagine how hard it would then be to leave the house without a filter. That happens and I have seen it.

Secondly, we have to ask why we are focusing on those people who seem perfect. It is not only a problem for our self-image but it limits our ability to think about those who have less. It is easy to look at beautiful people, as we are all drawn to beauty, but we need to be reminded to look at others with charity as well. It is not the shiny, wealthy people that we should focus on but those that the religions always direct us towards, those with less. The more time we spend thirsting over those who have more than us, the less time we have for those who don't.

When I focus my perspective on those who have less rather than those who seem to have more, I find I feel a sense of gratitude for what I have and greater potential to help those who have less. I am not thinking about what I lack but what I can give. I feel good because I can do good and that is an antidote to powerlessness and essential to living fearlessly. So I try to have perspective, to see how lucky I am and ask 'Why me?' about the good things as well as the bad, to use new perspectives which build empathy rather than staying within my own and developing jealousy.

So I want to make a suggestion that I think will help you to develop a positive perspective. Don't worry, I'm not telling you to unfollow @superyachtsofinstagram or @ijustwokeuplikethis because hopefully by doing this you will be able to see those images for what they are: tailored snapshots of single moments in the lives of a tiny minority. No, I want to suggest that you balance out each thought of envy, *'I wish I was like . . . '* with a thought of gratitude, *'I'm grateful that . . . '* because you will probably find that you are fortunate in many ways and feel happier and more capable the more you dwell on it. This will not only make you happier, but it will make you more fearless. Envy and doubt create fears in all of us that we have less and probably deserve less than those we idolise, whereas when you see your fortune, when you realise you are lucky, you will approach your dreams from a position of strength, safe in the knowledge that you are already beautiful and already rich. That is the power of looking for a new perspective.

I found that during my trip to Sierra Leone in 2022. I hadn't been since I was eight, when I walked to the gates of my grandma's house one morning and found a crowd of about 50 schoolchildren waiting to see their first little person. That experience and a few others had made me apprehensive about returning on this trip. I knew that disabled people face challenges in Sierra Leone that we don't in the UK and I worried that I'd feel even more awkward and different from the crowd than I do at home (shout out to chapter one! I'm still working on living by all my own commandments). What I found, though, was exactly the opposite: it was in moments when I realised how similar I was to other people that my perspective and my gratitude really grew. Meeting people who were so similar to me, and yet who, by virtue of their place of birth, received so much less support than I do was a powerful learning curve and it is one of the reasons people often give for travel as a powerful influence on their perspective and sense of gratitude.

I've never been rich but I've never been without the things I need to get by, and yet still there have been times in my life where I've had the envy mindset. I've wondered why I can't have a car, or my own flat, or the new clothes that other people seem to constantly buy, and those thoughts often led me to feel dissatisfied. That changed when I was in Sierra Leone and I met people who lacked the things I take for granted but appreciated so many things in life that I was failing to. They made me question how I could let the difference between having enough and having *loads* cause me unhappiness when they lack so much that I have and keep appreciating life and the good things that come for free?

The people that I met in Sierra Leone had the opposite mindset to the men you see on the Tube in London, heading into a well-paid job in the City with a screw face on. You have one group with all the things that money can buy and none of the time or energy to enjoy them, and another with no material wealth and their eyes wide open to the great things about being alive. I gained perspective in Sierra Leone and I realised that I need to be grateful for the essential things that I can buy, unaffected by the material things that I can't and ready to enjoy those things that can't be bought – things like laughter, dance and friendship. You don't need to be rich to be happy but you need to be happy for your life to be rich.

Wow, I'm coming off like a life coach here I know, but you don't buy a book about commandments for some lightweight suggestions so I'm going to assume you are down for the deep thoughts. So here's my second realisation about perspective that my trip to Sierra Leone gave me. While the first was not to let my happiness be affected by what others have, this was more about gratitude for the things I have been given. You see, a lot of people ask you for money in Freetown. It is understandable, as around half the population live on less than £1 a day, so when people approached me in the street it was because they knew that my small gift could make a large difference in their life. That didn't stop it becoming frustrating at times, though. You can tell I'm no life coach because I still struggle with all the commandments that

I'm laying out here, and at certain points during my trip, when the attention became too much, I just asked people to leave me alone. On the day that changed me it was a group of young disabled people that I waved away. I had been followed by a few different people that morning who had been asking me for money and I'd had enough of feeling like I had a target on my back. It is hard to describe, and might make me sound like a bad person, but I was frustrated that people seemed to just see me as an English person with cash to burn (maybe that's another way we can sympathise with those people we talked about envying earlier on? Maybe they get tired of being the subject of other people's envy?). So I walked on when the boys with disabilities asked me to stop. As I turned away, one spoke up and said, 'You're not any different to us you know.'

His words hit me from below. I knew immediately that he was right. These were young disabled Black people, people who I like to believe I stand up for in the UK from time to time, people whose voices I want to amplify, and I had just walked straight past when they asked for help. I turned back and spoke with them some more – explaining that I had been wrong to ignore them.

After we had left one another, I thought more about the interaction and the new perspective that the boy had given me joined my own. I began to develop my understanding and question things that I had taken for granted. What if I had been born in Sierra Leone? It was not a great stretch to imagine it – if my mum and dad had stayed, if they'd been there through the civil war and I'd grown up without the NHS to support me and the solid income my parents earned from their jobs within it, I could easily be sitting with that crew right there. I would have been asking the Westerners for help. I saw that it only takes a few small changes, a few 'sliding doors' moments for our lives to be like those of others that we choose to ignore. It also only takes a few small changes to step out of our ignorance.

I wish I hadn't needed those boys to help me understand their perspective but I was grateful they had. As a result, I became more grateful for the NHS that had given me steroids and physio as a child, who removed the fluid from my nose and brain that could have left me in a coma, and that there was this beautiful institution where my parents pursued fulfilling careers and that put food on our table. I'm grateful to those boys and I hope

I can do something for them one day. My plan is to return to Sierra Leone in some capacity and turn the opportunities I have had into opportunities for other disabled people who don't have the things that I used to take for granted.

I realise that is heavy but the way that travelling changes your perspective doesn't always have to be. In fact, in many cases, the greatest benefit of travel is a reminder that there is a big, interesting world out there and plenty of fun to be had. That is important to remember when you aren't enjoying the place you are in. In the last chapter, I talked about that period of my life when I was fearful that my dreams would always stay out of reach and that the place I was in would never be enough. I know it sounds basic but the best cure for that frustration was to be somewhere else. When I travelled, I reminded myself that there was always somewhere else, something else, and even if my office life felt like too much and not enough at the same time (I'll need more than an accounting degree to do the maths on that one), it wasn't *everything*. I could be sure of that fact because I basically left to go travelling with the circus . . .

OK, that maybe doesn't do it justice. I told you about how I was working in the club, dancing and meeting all these amazing people, but I didn't tell you about how we went on tour just before Covid hit. I want you to stop and picture this for a second: three tattooed gymnasts, a giant and a group of performers even smaller than me getting off a plane in New Delhi, India. Can you imagine what the scenes were like? We were mobbed. Loads of the people outside the airport had never seen a Black person. Most of them had never seen a little person. None of them had seen a seven-foot strongman flanked by a four-foot Black girl and a three-foot man rolling through with a group of tatted-up contortionists. The people in India didn't hold back. We would walk through the streets and get MOBBED; I kid you not – Justin Bieber 2011 mobbed, BTS on their last tour mobbed, The Beatles 1968 mobbed. It was like a group of oddly shaped performers had just won the Cricket World Cup, *Love Island* and *The Great Indian Bake Off* all at once and returned to Delhi airport on a private jet. We had to get security. I loved it.

India gave me a reminder that for all my life at the time felt stale, grey and predictable, there are places that are just the opposite. It reminded me that it wasn't the *world* that was boring, it was the time, place and situation I was in, and changing your place and path is easier than changing something as big and abstract as 'your world'. You even see it in the way we use the word 'world' – there's a mistake. We might use it to say, 'He's my world' or 'My world feels pretty small right now', but what we mean is 'my situation'. When you realise that, you see that it is much easier to change your situation than change the *whole world*. When you believe the place you're in is all there is, you can feel trapped, afraid and like there is nowhere to go, but when you *do go,* you gain a new perspective and see that you are in just one place of many and the life you are leading is just one possible version of your life. That is the power of travel and the power of perspective.

It is a strange truth that having a small perspective leads to far more fear than a broad one. You might expect that a larger perspective, with knowledge of all the challenges and risks that exist out there, would make you more fearful. But that is just not the case. With a limited perspective, believing that the place you are in is the only place you can be, you can feel suffocated, and I think that can be the most frightening thing of all.

The dancers and I travelled to Bangalore and then Mumbai after Delhi and it was great. You can feel an energy in India that I am so down for. Maybe it was just that the people I met there knew how to have fun. Whatever it was, I loved it and when I came back to my job in the office, I felt revitalised. I was going to be a performer and I was going to get out of there. Even if my first plan didn't work out, I was sure as hell going to come up with a second. It made me feel fearless, knowing that I had options and places to go. That is why I treat new perspectives as a path towards fearlessness, because anything big and frightening seems less so when seen with a wider lens: with distance, fear is shown for how small it is.

Our travelling troupe also took another trip after India, to Kosovo. I really got to know the rest of my team during that trip but it was two of my fellow performers that I really grew to love and who changed my perspective. The first was Anton, the seven-foot guy I mentioned, who is literally the biggest person I have ever seen. He's a super kind and gentle soul, and travelling with him gave me a new perspective on the challenges that I had faced. Anton gets similar treatment to me: people stare and ask how tall he is, and often make assumptions about his character based on nothing more than a passing glance. His height obviously also provides different challenges to mine. People don't always feel comfortable to press me about my size, to ask many questions or remind me of my difference, but with extremely tall people it seems to be different. Everyone wants to ask him about his height, whether he bangs his head a lot or if he has a 'normal-sized' girlfriend. His height presents him with difficulties, but people seem less careful around them than they are in my case, where there is a clear disability. That recognition of our similarities and differences was an interesting moment in extending my perspective. We couldn't be more different in appearance but aspects of our experience are similar. Before, I had always thought that the taller you are, the easier life gets. But now I saw that was simply not the case. I guess it makes sense that a tall man helped to raise my perspective!

The other friend who I became close with was certainly not a tall man but he elevated my understanding in a similar way to Anton. His name is Kane and he also has a form of dwarfism. Kane and I performed together in a part of the show which (ironically enough) played with people's perspectives. Our group had so much variety that the sheer difference between performers was a spectacle in its own right: one moment, an audience member would feel tiny beside Anton and the next, Kane or I would appear and they would have a sense of growing huge. It was a bit like *Alice in Wonderland* and I think a sense of wonder is part of what the creator of the show was trying to impart. It never felt exploitative and there was always respect, so I loved the experience of being in a show that played with people's expectation and perspective.

Working with Kane actually had an interesting impact on my own perspective. By being around him, I got an understanding of why taller people sometimes do things to me that I find challenging. For example, I have often found it really frustrating when people bend down to talk to me – particularly when their approach to the conversation has a patronising tone. I'm like, 'I'm small, fool, not young.' But at times when I was talking to Kane, I found myself doing it as he is smaller than me. I was like, 'No, Fats! Check yourself! You can't start being patronising because you are now the *second* smallest in the room!' But actually, it was really useful because that shift in perspective gave me empathy for people who had behaved that way towards me and an understanding that maybe they weren't always trying to patronise me, just trying to make sure that they could hear me.

The other thing I found myself doing with Kane was being protective. I know, right? I had a seven-foot strongman behind me and I was stepping ahead, clearing the way through crowds for Kane because he was a few inches smaller than me. It's pretty hilarious when I think about it. It was just a reflex reaction; we'd be in the club and I'd put my hand on his head to try to make sure people didn't bump into him. People had done that to me so many times and it had always annoyed me, yet here I was playing the tall saviour to a friend! When I realised what I was doing I apologised and he was super cool, but it was another big shift in perspective. I can see now that people being protective of me isn't the result of some deep-seated opinion they have of me, it's just a care reflex and not intended as an insult.

So working with Kane and Anton gave me new perspectives on my experience but it also taught me something more general: we can all be a victim and we can all be an offender. Nothing about our life or our experience means we will never fall foul of the mistakes that we have seen other people make, so we should be prepared to give them the benefit of the doubt when they make them. I mean, if I can patronise someone for being small then anything is possible.

So the big question is, how do these shifts in perspective make us more fearless? I think there are a few really important ways. One is that when we see the world from a new perspective, we realise that it is not the same thing as 'our world' and we can start to see our own situation more as something we can change and improve. Secondly, when we see the world from other people's perspectives, we see ourselves differently. We realise that we can change and grow, and that always fills me with a sense of potential. Third, when we take on board new perspectives, we see other people through their own eyes and we develop empathy, which makes us both more understanding and forgiving.

And forgiving is one of the most fearless things we can do.

The Timbo Takeaway

When you see the world your perspective grows, and when you try to see other people's perspectives your world does too. So take time to think about people who have less than you and try not to fixate on people who have more, because it might be an illusion. Remember to be grateful for the things you have but see the world and be aware of all the things it can offer – you might just realise that there are places and things that make you happy which you just haven't found yet. Finally, if the place you are in is not one in which you are happy, then there is a big world out there and the more you see, the more you will know about where else you could be.

I'll see you on the beach somewhere . . . Or in the rainforest . . . Or on the mountain top. Try them all and see which you enjoy.

Reflections

Have you ever met anyone who made you think differently about your own life? How?

Think about someone you have been envious of. Consider the challenges they could have faced in their life that you might not be aware of.

Think about a type of landscape you would like to see – it could be mountains, deserts, jungles or cities. Now look up examples of that kind of place. Think about going there and what you would like to do if you did. It may not be possible right now but it can be someday, so start getting ready!

....
....
....
....
....
....
....
....
....
....

**YOU DON'T NEED TO
BE RICH TO BE HAPPY
BUT YOU NEED TO
BE HAPPY FOR YOUR
LIFE TO BE RICH.**

COMMANDMENT 7:

Stop

When your dreams come true, it can happen so fast that you hardly notice. Stop and take a look around because it may be happening to you right now.

Writing this book has been a real learning curve. I have had to stop and process the experiences in my life that have got me to where I am today and that have really impacted me. The thing that has surprised me most is how that has helped me to understand myself in ways that I would never have expected. For example, I hadn't really thought about how my experiences of bullying shaped my perspective until I took time to put it into words and I don't believe I really understood how important self-belief has been in my journey until I tried to explain it to you. I have also started to see more with each passing chapter how my commandments all build on similar foundations but take different shapes when applied in different situations. The message here, to stop and take a moment to look around, reflects this.

You will remember (and if you don't – flick back; I've made this book so you can come back to different chapters when you need to) the commandment of chapter four was 'Trust the Journey'. We discussed how important it is to be present during times where you are hustling, to never wish away the struggle and to enjoy the moments in which you are striving. Now I want to take that idea of appreciating the moment and extend it to situations where things seem to be going well – because, trust me, sometimes you can be so caught up in that hustler's mindset that you don't even notice when your dreams are coming true around you.

The challenge of appreciating the things we have already achieved and the beauty of the place we are in while also staying focused on our goals is real. I think it is one of the reasons why successful people so often struggle with their happiness, which can seem like a massive lack of gratitude from the outside. When we are striving for something it often seems as if achieving that goal will be the key to satisfaction and contentment. But in reality, if we haven't developed the skill of appreciating the moment, we probably won't be able to value our success when we get there. Until we realise that true success comes from being present and enjoying the moment, we will always be struggling for something, no matter how successful we may appear to be.

If I'm completely honest, the call to stop and appreciate what you have achieved may be the commandment I need most right now, given where I am in my life. Things have gone to plan over the last couple of years and at times, I need reminding of that fact and to stop and value the things that I have.

In a strange way, I felt more comfortable when I was only beginning to get recognition than I do now. As the six months of striving to establish myself on social media came to a close, I felt a clear purpose and a clear identity – I was a growing creator. There weren't huge expectations and although there weren't that many rewards, I felt that I was part of a community who were branching out on a new platform. Sometimes, these days, as my career has moved forward, I just feel like the challenges grow and the competition does too, like I'm a formerly big fish who has jumped to a much bigger pond. We'll get on to that, though. First, we need to talk about breaking through, how all the striving and planning gave this big-little fish a wave wavy enough that she could ride on out of that puddle I called office life. The waiting room phase of my career.

Before I really committed to online comedy and activism, I tried to create other opportunities for myself in creative spaces. My first gig was a music video which I worked on between weekend shifts at the club. I got paid £60 for a day's filming and felt like a boss. I followed that up by running my own dance class. The weeks of planning for that and the execution netted me a hefty £30. It's lucky I wasn't in it for the money because, speaking as an accountant, those jobs were not necessarily worth the time! Fortunately, I was very much trying *not* to speak like an accountant – I was trying to move like a performer and from that perspective, the work seemed good. I also gave a talk at an event celebrating the Sierra Leonean diaspora, which felt incredibly powerful. I mean, I could probably have hopped on a mic in front of 15 Sierra Leonean women any day of the week – I would have just needed to go on one of my mum's WhatsApp groups – but this time I was asked and it felt like *I was in demand.*

So when lockdown hit and the events dried up, I tried to put the energy I had reserved for performance into my online comedy. In late May 2020, three months after starting on TikTok, I had my first breakthrough. I had been relentless, posting every day, putting my spin on any and every possible trend and sound, but that day I noticed a trend that seemed perfect. People were making all these different videos about the year 2020. They were treating it like a character, one who had let down all the other years before and after. I knew I had to jump on it. Even though the pandemic year had been OK for me and the lockdown had saved me from the daily drudge of office life, I knew I could make something funny. So I created a routine around a Tyra Banks monologue from *America's Next Top Model*. It was a moment when she lost it at one of the contestants and gave them a real dressing-down. I felt like 2020 needed a bit of Tyra Banks so I posted it that evening and waited.

When I woke up my phone was overheating. I could literally feel it pulsating beside my head. I unlocked it and when I opened up the app I saw the numbers, hundreds of thousands of views and likes from every corner of the globe. I had been used to my videos racking up a couple of hundred likes, but now I now had a 30-second clip with as many viewers as the population of Iceland (and I don't mean the shop).

It was exhilarating, I was bouncing off the walls, refreshing the page to see how many eyes worldwide had watched me playing the characters of 2018, 2019 and 2020 since I had last checked, and each time the jump in numbers shocked me. As I settled down to bed that night I felt really satisfied but decided to refresh just one more time to get a final count. When the screen reloaded I saw . . . nothing. The video had been taken down for a copyright infringement. I was ready to storm TikTok's head office with my Icelandic warrior army behind me, but then I stopped. As I thought about it, I realised that it wasn't *that video* that mattered but the fact that I did it, that I could do it and that I would do it again.

So instead of mourning the lost video, I logged back on the next day and I tried to bring the same energy to the next one. That was an important lesson for me: not to be fixated on individual achievements or numbers but to see them as a validation of the process. If you have achieved something, no one can really take it away from you because the record or the award is not the achievement, it was the doing it. So I stopped for a moment to appreciate what I had achieved and then I did it again – I made another video. Then again and again, and at the end of that month, my following had grown into the hundreds of thousands. Rather than losing time thinking about the video I had lost, I used the confidence it gave me to create momentum to make more. At that point, I felt like the sky was the limit – but I wasn't even ready for the reaction to my next video.

It was so simple, but as soon as I finished it I knew that it was perfect. 'How to Get a Guy' was the tagline. I won't go through it in detail as I'm sure you can find it (and detailed descriptions of funny faces are never as good as the faces themselves), but I can tell you that when I posted it I felt like something was going to happen. A lot more happened than I expected. It hit 11 million views overnight. That's just unreasonable. I was sure there must have been an accounting error, a zero in the wrong place, but once I checked I realised that, apart from my career choice at the time, there were no accounting errors in the building. The number was right. From that video and others, my following jumped from 100,000 to 500,000 in a month. I knew then that I had an audience, an opportunity to speak out and be heard, but I also had new expectations. I could feel the pressure rising, but when I stopped to think about it, I knew I could rise with it.

It was strange, though. Everything on my

phone suggested a lot had changed but nothing in my physical world had. It was like I was leading a double life, or I was some boss character in a metaverse that didn't really exist. The pandemic meant that there were no events, no chances to meet anyone who had enjoyed my work, and I still wasn't getting any paid jobs. I was sitting at home getting hassled about flopping in my accounting job and not one Icelandic person had told me I was doing great in the real world. I knew I couldn't dwell on it, though; it would be a mistake to focus on what I didn't have in that moment when so many things I had been desperate for were happening all around me.

That is a funny feature of perspective: so often we can feel disappointed at outcomes that we would have been desperate for previously because we see how they could be even better. Maybe you have had a similar experience. Perhaps you were revising for your exams and praying to pass, and then when the Bs that you would have been desperate for at the start of your revision period came through, you wished that some of them were As. It is good in those moments to stop and remember how you felt along the way, to let your past self give your present one a pep talk . . . or a slap in the face. My past self was saying, 'Come on, Fatima, you can't be annoyed that your online success isn't translating into real-world outcomes yet. Six months ago you (*that's me*) would kill to be where you are at now!' I had to be realistic. So I didn't let the fact that my success was mainly online or the lack of any income from it get to me.

The main thing was that I could feel myself rising to the challenge of being a creator. I had been on TikTok for four months and I was getting good at it — I was posting like clockwork, ideas were flowing and I had even begun to start discussing my disability more online. That might not seem like a big milestone but trust me, it was. All my life I had been a proud person but I had never wanted to get any *more* attention for my disability than that which naturally comes my way. If people I trusted wanted to talk about my perspectives or opinions on matters relating to my circumstances then that was fine, but the idea of openly discussing disability issues with people I didn't know felt completely new. I realised, though, that I had a platform and I felt like the people who were following me seemed to come to me with love. So I began to put up some explainers — just short, fun attempts to explain aspects of my life and my disability that might give my followers a chance to learn something. That was a huge step. If you remember, at college, I wouldn't even *approach* people who hadn't approached me out of fear that they may be judgemental or critical of me or my disability, and here I was explaining the challenges of dwarfism and pregnancy to 500,000 people online. It was a shift and it was only possible because my self-esteem had grown, but I have to admit that making that shift online certainly helped. For all that the internet and social media get a bad rap for distorting people's perspectives and breaking down social connections, it can be a really powerful tool for people whose voices have been diminished in the outside world. When you have had challenges in face-to-face interactions because of your identity, the internet can provide a safe space for you to speak up. You can reach millions and you can gain support that you never knew existed. Plus, unlike in the real world, you can literally *block out the haters*.

I don't know whether it was due to my effort to start speaking out about disability or simply the fact that my following had grown, but I got my first paid job online around that time. It was a YouTube show called 'Shake My Beauty' and

I do think that my willingness to speak openly about beauty norms and disability influenced the decision of the creators to cast me. It wasn't a huge amount of money but it encouraged me to push on over the next few months and be more outspoken. So I did. I worked harder and at the end of those months, in the last week of my six-month plan, I got fired.

Yeah, I got fired. The company I was working for had the *nerve* to tell me I was more focused on my social media channels than my job in their team. I mean, *come on*, you've listened to me – does it sound like that was the case? OK, yes, it was absolutely the case and they were right to fire my uncommitted ass. It was August, we had been in lockdown for nearly half a year and I was getting ready to leave anyway, so my priorities were pretty clear. The pandemic had shaken things up and now I was starting to see where the pieces were falling, so I felt good about it. My parents on the other hand were, let's say, *undecided*. They were a little less positive about me getting fired, to the point of even being a bit concerned. The numbers beside my videos didn't mean much to them and the fact that I had earned as much on social media in six months as I did in a week as an accountant didn't convince them that my sacking was a cause for celebration. They had made their minds up. I needed to get another job.

This time, though, I dug my heels in. I was close to making a career out of this – I could feel it and I needed them to understand. I even drafted in an auntie to make my case. She had seen my work on social media and she knew that it wouldn't be long before I could support myself. Between the two of us, we convinced them. That, my friend, is the power of aunties. Like blades on a Swiss army knife, there is an auntie for every situation. This time, I called on social-media auntie (a rare and lesser-spotted variety) to provide me with intergenerational backing. With her help, my parents agreed I could have two months to focus solely on socials, living on savings. At the end of that time, it would provide me with enough income to stand on my own two feet and if it didn't then the job hunt would start again. I know they just wanted me to have security and even now they still want me to have a back-up plan, but they also know that I am pretty single-minded. If I have made a decision, they can trust me to follow through and pursue it with a fierce dedication. So I approached those next two months as a creator with a job-search mentality. I kept grinding but I also got some representation to help me get paid work and I made sure to keep believing that I belonged.

That feeling of doing well and doubting whether you deserve it, of wondering if maybe you have just got lucky and everyone else has made a mistake by believing in you, is known as impostor syndrome. It's self-doubt for the self-made, a strange negative reaction to things going well, and I think it is an important thing to unpack, given the message of this chapter. In my opinion, the worst thing we can do when things go well for us is to let ourselves believe that it is just luck, that soon enough we'll be found out as a fraud.

But do you know what? I think everyone is an impostor in some way. No one *really* knows what they are doing, from the smallest baby to the biggest, most official and officious official. We are all just trying to do our best and anyone who acts like they always absolutely know what they are doing is just a better salesperson than the rest of us. I mean, look at Boris Johnson. You remember him? Blond guy? Talked a lot of rubbish? If there is anyone who should know what they are doing it is the one making decisions for the whole country, but that guy seemed to get by with pure self-confidence. He just blagged and kept blagging. If he'd had even one ounce of self-consciousness he would have been dragged down in a wave of impostor syndrome so large it would have taken out a whole country with him. But he believed that he deserved to be successful, to be powerful and to be where he was. Maybe that was just his personality and maybe it was his upbringing, but it shows that nothing propels you forward more than self-belief and nothing holds you back more than self-imposed doubt.

There definitely seems to be a social element to impostor syndrome. As a rule, women are more likely to experience it and I think people in historically marginalised communities can feel it more too. We don't take it for granted that we get to be seen, that we get to be successful, so when we do achieve we are more likely to think that there has been some sort of mistake, another accounting error or positive discrimination at play. Well, my friends, take it from me − if there is a mistake, roll with it. If you are in the building, you belong there and if you think that maybe you are the only one who sees how clueless you are then maybe you are the one who is wrong. Everyone seemed to think that BoJo was a top fool but he didn't, and with only that self-belief he managed to keep being the prime minister for a long time. So who's the fool there?

I mention impostor syndrome because the message of this chapter is to stop and take stock when things go well, but also that we should do so *positively*. There is no good to working hard for a goal and then stopping to think about how little we deserve it when it arrives. That is self-sabotage and it is an even worse use of our time than not stopping to reflect at all. At least if you are mindlessly pursuing the next goal and then the next one, you are not trying to trip yourself up. Impostor syndrome both stops you preparing your next steps *and* makes you doubt every one that has taken you to where you are. It is not always easy to believe that you belong but remember: if you have made it there, then you do.

Having a talent management agency behind me helped me to drop some of my impostor syndrome. The simple fact that a group of people believed in what I was doing enough to give their time and effort to be part of the process was hugely empowering, and for someone who had only really experienced validation in an online space it made a big difference. It meant that even when well-paid jobs didn't arrive as a result of my creations, I kept believing that I was worth the effort.

Then, just as my parents were starting to lose patience, leaving tabs with job searches open on the desktop and starting odd conversations over the dinner table about how interesting nine-to-five jobs can actually be, I got a proper paid gig. The shoe brand Schuh *(geddit?)* asked me to be part of a campaign that they were doing around inclusivity. I had a chance to speak up on my motivation, discuss the challenges I face and pursue new opportunities . . . and I got paid to dance and wear cool shoes. It felt good to me and it really validated the effort I had made to showcase more of my personality and speak honestly in my videos. I knew it wasn't a one-off and from there I just kept building.

The years since I broke through have been fun. I've been on TV and on the radio, I'm making a podcast and possibly moving into acting jobs. I just keep believing that anyone who approaches me believes in me and that there is no reason I shouldn't do the same. No matter how big the stage gets, I can grow to fill it. That is my approach to impostor syndrome in a nutshell. I cannot control whether other people believe in me, I can only make sure to keep believing in myself. That is particularly important when I feel the pressure that comes from having a platform.

Now that I have established myself, there is not only a risk of impostor syndrome but burnout from the desire to keep growing at the rate I have so far. That can be hard, as you can't predict how people will react to your work or guarantee that every day your progress will outstrip the last. I try to stop and take stock – to remind myself that I cannot let my achievements so far become a weight of expectation around my neck. I wouldn't give up my progress for the world but equally, I cannot give up my world in the name of progress. I have to remember not to tie my self-worth to the number of followers that I am gaining (or not gaining . . .) and I cannot believe I am any better or worse for my successes or failures. We are all valuable simply for being ourselves and what we achieve or don't achieve doesn't change that. So staying true to myself benefits me both in terms of my mental health and my work, because I believe that honesty is something that my followers appreciate. I am unique and if that is working well in the public sphere then that is fine, but the approach and the self-belief cannot change if the reactions do.

The commandment that covers all the

experiences and lessons that I have outlined in this chapter, though, is to stop and appreciate the moment. If I ever doubt myself or worry that I am not progressing as planned, I take a look at where I am and remember that my dreams have already come true. It is too easy to let our expectations rise and our fears grow and to lose sight of that fact. If you don't stop and look around, you might not notice that you already have so many of the things that you once dreamed of.

The Timbo Takeaway

Being present and appreciating the journey is as important when things are going well as when they are not. We often work hard towards a goal and fail to give ourselves a moment to appreciate it when it is achieved. Even worse, we can raise our expectations and place new pressures on ourselves when we have progressed. It is important to remind ourselves where we have come from and appreciate what we have.

We should also never lose sight of who we are. We are all always valuable just by being ourselves and we don't become any more or less valuable when things go well or badly. If we remember that, then we can separate our identity from our achievements and be stronger in the face of our disappointments. You 'made it' the second you came into this world and you will have made it on the day you leave. So on every day in between, you should try to do your best and remember that nothing can change your value and no person should make you see it differently.

Reflections

Think about a time when you worked hard towards something. Maybe it was a work project or the end of a school year. How soon was it before you started thinking about the next one? How quickly did you forget your pride in the achievement when your next challenge came along? Look back on that achievement and see if you can bring up the enjoyment of that moment again.

Have you ever felt impostor syndrome? Done well and doubted whether you deserve it? Look back at those times and ask yourself whether any good came from it. Did anyone ever turn up to say that, actually, you were right and didn't deserve to be there? Or did you just keep getting better from there? Write out what you would say to yourself if you were your own best friend in that situation. What would you tell yourself to make you believe that you deserve everything you have achieved?

Stop and think about your life right now. What are you grateful for? What is the fortune that you have which you sometimes forget about in the moment? What would you five years ago say if they saw you now and the things you have achieved?

NO ONE REALLY KNOWS WHAT THEY ARE DOING ...

FROM THE SMALLEST BABY TO THE BIGGEST, MOST OFFICIAL AND OFFICIOUS OFFICIAL.

COMMANDMENT 8:

Love You

Learn to love yourself, and then someone else.

It's funny. With all the love that exists in the world, people still act like they know nothing about it. Look at musicians: love is the main subject of their songs and all they seem to have is questions. I'm serious – turn on your radio now and I bet all you'll hear is singers asking for help to work out what is going on in their hearts.

What Is Love? (Baby don't hurt me)
What's Love Got to Do with It?
Where Is the Love?
I Wanna Know What Love Is

Well Tina, will.i.am, . . . erm, the guy who sang 'I Wanna Know What Love Is' – I'm not sure I want to tell you because I tuned in for a mellow magic moment, not a Q&A. I'm not saying all love songs have been good for nothing. There's plenty of good music about heartbreak, longing and rage, but I'm not sure all the books and pop songs in the world are getting us any closer to understanding, feeling or maintaining love. They just help us feel the frustrations around it more intensely, with the help of a banging disco beat or half-rapped verse from Fergie along the way. So I've decided that this book actually has to offer some useful advice about love, for you and for others, because it's become pretty clear that we can't rely on Haddaway or Bieber ('What Do You Mean?') because they don't seem to know.

So there it is, I've laid out my cards. All the love songs in the world aren't going to help you find love (only 'A Million Love Songs' – thanks Take That) but fortunately, I have learned some lessons along the way that might, and all of them start with learning to love yourself. That is because learning to love yourself is true love and the basis of all other kinds. It's the sort of love that no one can break up. A guaranteed lifelong relationship, like swans or penguins have. The kind of love that will actually teach you enough to answer all the silly questions that pop stars keep asking (that's what I mean, Justin).

That has been the case in my life. I've struggled with low expectations and high ones, excitement and disappointment; I've made good choices and bad, but the most powerful force in all of those experiences has been my approach to myself. When I am good to myself, when I back and love myself, I love others better and I find that I am more than capable of helping them to love me. When the opposite has been true, when I have been uncertain or undervalued myself, the best I could hope for was a single life and the worst a relationship based on my self-doubt.

For many people, our first experience of love comes from our family and our earliest relationship is usually with our parents or carers. This can be a source of strength or a problem, depending on our home environment growing up. If you were mainly shown insecure relationships as a child they may well seem normal. When our parents model dysfunctional relationships (often because one or both of them is struggling with their own self-love) then we can end up building our relationships to look like theirs. I was fortunate that, even in the face of many challenges I had as a child, I always had a secure home life and parents who modelled a good relationship. That allowed me to face my own relationship challenges with a secure sense of self and safety and provided an example of the sort of healthy relationship that I wanted to find, even if it never seemed to be on the horizon.

My mum and dad were never lovey-dovey but they showed their love for one another by always making an effort to spend time together and performing little acts of kindness that made each other's lives easier. My dad would always pick my mum up from work, for example, or she would try to cook his favourite meals if he had a bad day. Small things like that are expressions of love in my eyes, and probably also just a good idea when trying to run a madhouse full of kids and their friends.

People show love and appreciate it being shown to them in different ways. This has been described through the idea of 'love languages' and I find it quite useful for understanding how people like to give and receive affection. Your love language is thought to be a combination of five different forms of communication and how you rank them in terms of your preference. These are:

- **Words of affirmation:** verbal expressions of love, support and kindness
- **Quality time:** dedicating time to being together
- **Physical touch:** holding hands, giving hugs or offering an arm around the shoulder
- **Acts of service:** doing something kind

and/or unexpected for your partner
- **Gifts:** giving something unexpected to the other person

The idea is that all of these things can be expressions of love, but that we place different importance on them depending on how we like to show and receive love. In my parents' case, they are both committed to quality time and acts of service. I don't know how they decided that those are the two that work for them but obviously, over 30 years they have found ways of expressing love for one another that work and understood that others they each need less – it is safe to say that 'words of affirmation' are not a big part of their love language as my parents prefer to 'walk the walk' rather than 'talk the talk' of love. In fact, I only heard my dad say that he loves my mum for the first time recently and it came as a shock. I'd *seen* that he loved her plenty over the years but I'd not heard him use the word. To many people, that would seem strange because they want their partner to show their love through words, but I think that just speaks to how different people can be in their expressions of love.

I think I used their love languages as an example

when I was searching for someone. I knew that I would like to have something like they do – all action, no talk – and whenever I ran into someone who talked the talk I was always wary. I guess that words of affirmation aren't big in my love language either because from my perspective, words are cheap.

The fact that my parents established a loving home was also important in the face of the challenges I ran up against. While the world outside could be an intimidating place for a young disabled girl, I could always be confident that I was returning to a place where I was loved and appreciated. Knowing about the experiences of my friends who grew up in the care system and never had that security made me aware of how difficult life could be without that support. It could be difficult to develop a positive self-image and self-love as someone who felt different in the playground and so I can only imagine how hard it could be for my disabled friends who returned to foster homes or care facilities where the security that I had wasn't a given. That security allowed me to develop an image of myself that reflected the perspective of the people around me who loved me. As an adult, I try to treat myself with the same love and affection that my family gave me and that has been key to facing challenges in all areas of life, including love, even if it could be one of the harder ones in which to maintain a loving self-image.

I think that the most important relationship we have is with ourselves. I don't mean that in a selfish way and I'm not promoting always putting our needs before those of others, but in my mind, you will never be able to establish a healthy relationship with another person if you haven't done so already with yourself. My approach is to treat myself like a loved one. I respect myself, I am kind, I try to be real with myself and I try to be forgiving. Many people have an internal dialogue with themselves that they wouldn't accept from a friend or colleague and that can be really damaging. If you had a friend who was constantly doubting you or telling you that you weren't good enough, you would be right to question that friendship – so it is always useful to question what your friendship with yourself is like. If you aren't kind to yourself and you don't show yourself respect, then it is unlikely that anyone else will either. My family and friends had to teach me that, and it is still something that I am working on. For a long time, I didn't stand up for myself and I didn't always have the self-love to convince myself that the cruel things that others said and did weren't true. Unless you believe in yourself, you'll start to believe what others say about you, and if you run into bullies or people who have their own damage that they want to project on you, that can be harmful.

Over time, though, with the help of my family and friends, I was able to develop a fairly strong sense of self. You'll remember from the bullying chapter that I got to a place where I did stand up for myself, but I found that I needed to grow even further to be prepared for the world of relationships. It is one thing to love yourself enough to stand up against bullying but another to make you stand up for yourself when people who you want to love you treat you poorly. That was a struggle for me as I grew into my teenage years and started to look for a relationship of my own.

When I was about 15, people I knew were beginning to get into relationships and I knew that I would like one for myself. I had just reached the point of realising that I didn't deserve to be a victim but looking back now, I can see that I was nowhere near believing that I deserved to be loved. The first giveaway is that I was surprised anyone ever found me attractive. I would sometimes get some interest or a compliment and I honestly felt like it was some sort of gift from on high, a miraculous event based on someone else's mistake. I would be so happy and shocked that I would take the compliment however and wherever it came. That can be a problem as attention can come for the wrong reasons – and in my case, the most common source of that problematic attention was a thing called fetishisation. I know it is a strange word and when you find out about it you may not be sure it presents a problem for you, but I think understanding fetishisation and how I grew past it as an issue in my life can actually be useful for all sorts of people.

So here it is – Fetishisation 101 (I bet auntie didn't think we'd be covering this when she got you my book for Christmas). Sometimes people make others an object of desire based on an aspect of their identity. That can be harmless and sometimes it is simply a reflection of preferences, as in 'I like tall guys' or 'I am attracted to larger women'. Obviously, we all have certain things that we find attractive about other people, so not all attractions to certain traits are fetishisations, but an attraction can stray into fetishisation if you are attracted to the aspect of a person's identity rather than the person themselves. In my case, people have fetishised my disability. This has come in the form of comments like 'I'd love to sleep with a little woman' or 'I'd like to be with a disabled girl'. You can probably immediately see the problem with comments like that. The person speaking is not interested in me but in being with someone (anyone?!?!) who has the same disability as me. That is a case of fetishisation and it is something I have come up against a lot in the past.

The reason it is important to discuss fetishisation and self-love is that when my self-esteem was low and I didn't feel love for myself, I thought fetishisation was the best that I could expect. In my teenage years, when I received those 'miraculous' compliments, usually I was being fetishised, but my self-esteem was so low that I thought I should be happy to receive any interest. I fundamentally didn't think I could be desirable, so even if the attraction someone felt for me seemed to come from a place of othering and fetishisation, I thought I was lucky. Now, as someone who has (spoiler alert) experienced proper love and who has learned to love myself, I understand that I could only be grateful for attention like that because I didn't feel like I deserved any attention at all. Good or bad.

It was also hard for me to separate attraction and fetishisation early on because my disability and my body are tied together so closely. In some ways, someone being attracted to my body *is* being attracted to my disability, because my body is that of a disabled woman. That made it hard to disentangle those cases where people were fetishising my disability from those where people were simply finding my body attractive – a body that is defined by my physical condition. This issue becomes clearer when described through the medium of my behind. My bottom. My booty. Achondroplasia and fantastic genes have come together to create a pretty significant offering in that department. If someone was to say that they like my bum, I would have that doubt in my mind about whether they like *my* bum or the type of bum I represent. Black, achondroplasic, young – any of those things could be a way in which someone was fetishising me. As I am sure you can see – it was a minefield.

This is not only a problem for people with disabilities. We all have things that we feel are more attractive than others, but no one would want a person to be interested in us *only because* of those aspects. You don't want someone who loves you just because you have big boobs, or you're rich, or East Asian, etc. You want to be loved for reasons that can't be put into such simple descriptions; you want to believe that your boobs or bank account or race could change and that it wouldn't impact the love that the other person feels for you. That is something we all deserve but it is hard to believe that it is going to happen when someone opens up a conversation on Tinder with 'I've nvr slept with a dwerf b4. Do u wnt 2 come round 2 mine tnite?'

No, Darren. I actually don't.

It might sound like a joke but it's not, because when I started trying to find love on dating apps that was actually my life. I began to use them when I was in sixth form. I'd never had any (genuine) interest from anyone around my area or school and I still didn't have the self-belief to approach people myself, so I decided that I would go online. My thinking was that it was a safer space, where I could save myself the pain of people patronising me and find men who were already potentially interested. What I found was plenty of interested men, but even more patronising behaviour and fetishisation. I knew it was a problem straight away as every conversation seemed to magically skip the date-discussing stage. We would say hello and within a few minutes, the person would be inviting me around to theirs like they were making a booking. It was only later that I realised the thinking beneath that. In their minds, because they were attracted to someone with a disability, they didn't need to go through the hassle of making me interested in them through dating. They thought they were doing me a favour, so at least I could do them the favour of going round to theirs before we had even had a conversation. It was really hard to take and I had to work so hard to remember that I deserved more and become patient enough to keep waiting until I got that.

But I know you wanted to be given some better advice than 'be patient'. Well, sorry my friend, I promised to do better than one of those love songs that offer quick fixes and fast love, so you'll have to settle for the Fats approach: love yourself and be patient. Those two ideas have been a bit of a theme of this book about fearlessness, because nothing is going to make you feel more fearful than doubting yourself or telling yourself that you are running out of time. You are enough and you have enough time. So be fearless, be a good friend to yourself and try to be patient.

I had to develop even greater patience on those

rare occasions when my Tinder conversations actually led to a date. Not all conversations ended as quickly as the one with Darren above, and I'm sorry to say that those that went further actually led to more disappointment. The alternative to someone suggesting a quick hook-up seemed to be getting slowly stood up. It happened multiple times. I would talk to a guy for ages, we would set a date, I would take a long journey into London and then . . . Stand alone for three hours outside a multiplex in Wood Green.

I'd be there twiddling my thumbs, hoping and believing that they had been in some sort of horrible accident (joking, but also a bit not joking) which was keeping them from arriving. I simply could not believe that they hadn't turned up. For me to have got as far as the date-organising stage meant that a lot of vetting had gone on: they had proved themselves not to be a perve (tick), been vaguely fun (tick) and seemed genuinely interested (ti . . . oh, cross actually). It was a low bar that I set and on every occasion my dates failed to reach it. I would try to understand their reasons for standing me up but in truth, it didn't do any good. I couldn't start creating theories about it based on my insecurities, so I just had to remember that if they weren't reliable enough for a first date then they wouldn't be reliable enough to have a relationship with.

Soon, though, my patience did sort of pay off. I say 'sort of' because I did find someone, but it didn't work out. This is the third category of disappointment, after 1. fetishisation and 2. being stood up, comes good ol' 3. non-committal situationship. You may have experienced this category too. You may have had all three, in which case I salute you on winning Fats Timbo's Dating Bingo (E4, where you at?). This 'situationship' (and I use that word because, as you will see, it was definitely not a relationship) lasted close to two years while I was at college. We got along well, he was undeniably not a weirdo, he turned up and we had fun together so, naturally, I thought he was a keeper (low self-esteem alert). After two years of seeing each other, though, I was starting to feel uncertain. I knew I liked him and we had been hanging out for a long time, but I wasn't sure he had any plans for a future together. So I went ahead and asked him – 'Do you see us together in five years?'

A long pause followed . . .

No answer.

So I cut it off. Then and there (high self-esteem

alert). If I wanted a long-term relationship with him but he didn't, and not only that but he didn't even have words to describe any kind of future together, then I knew I had to cut my losses. I had waited long enough to find a relationship and I had dedicated enough time to him to expect some kind of commitment. But now I knew that he couldn't give it to me, I had to move on. I'm proud I did that. People often stick with something that isn't great just because they have already invested so much time and effort into it, and that can be a big mistake. Just because you have spent your past on something that isn't working, it doesn't mean you have to give your future up to it as well.

So it was back to the apps. Back to the weird opening lines and being stood up, back to step one. That was hard but I knew I was better off on the starting line of a journey that was going places than halfway along one that wasn't. I won't bore you with all the failures because I know you want to hear about the time that worked out, but I think it is important to note that I really grew as a person after the situationship ended. During that time, I figured out what I wanted to do with my life and my confidence grew far beyond anything that my teenage self would have recognised. I became a woman and I began to love myself. Then, I grew towards a place where I could truly be loved.

When I first met Alan online I didn't know what to expect. I'd never had anything close to a positive experience with the apps so I went in with a healthy sense of realism. He was just another guy who I liked the look of but who could easily just turn out to be another disappointment. But when we got to talking it did seem different. Our conversations were genuine and we really quickly found that we had a number of shared interests. We both loved dance, music and film-making, and I enjoyed our chats over the app so much that I went straight in and asked if we could talk over the phone. He says that was a first for him, having a woman move so quickly, but it became clear that it was the right thing to do. We spoke for hours on the phone about our lives and our plans, and, before we knew it, we had arranged a date. He was living in West London at the time and I felt like going into town so we met up near where he lived.

The connection was just as good in person. Obviously, there were some first date nerves and a couple of awkward moments, but I knew we were hitting it off. At the end of the date, the moment felt right and I was sure he was going to kiss me. Then he didn't and my alarm bells started to go off. We went our separate ways and I became certain that he hadn't made the move because he wasn't attracted to me, that it was a sign he saw us more as friends. Looking back now, I see I was self-sabotaging. As much as my self-esteem had grown, I wasn't prepared to be disappointed by someone who seemed really great, so I went straight in and invented the disappointment for myself. At least that way, I could control it. It was an error but all of my bad experiences had led me to believe that this was just too good to be true. I still didn't have the self-love to believe that someone like him could love me back and I think my experience of guys being really forward had warped my perceptions.

So I ghosted him. I'm ashamed to admit it but I hid myself away from the potential disappointment and we didn't go out again. We still followed each other online and from time to time we would like each other's work, but in my mind, the moment had gone. Then one day, as my videos were growing in popularity, I put out a request for someone to help me with editing. He was the first person to reply. He would do it. I was unsure if it was a mistake to mix a past romance with work, but I also knew that he was a really good editor. So I put my doubts aside and decided that we could be a good fit professionally. So we started talking again whenever I needed to work on a video and gradually, we found that the conversations were even better than they had been at first. We talked about our work and lives, about succeeding as disabled people in a world that isn't well designed for us. We got along, basically, and our work together was seamless so we decided to keep it up. Alan suggested that we have a business meeting to discuss our approach. That sounded reasonable to me. I was a professional woman and now I had someone to work with, it seemed like a good idea.

Little did I know that he was planning another move. We met at a cafe in Fulham, a really beautiful spot on a sunny autumn day. As soon as I arrived, he gave me a massive hug and pulled out a present. The gap between me realising that this was a date rather than a business meeting and being really happy about it was about half a second. I didn't feel tricked, I felt chuffed. He treated me really well and we spent the whole day together. We ate and walked his dog, and generally spent the sort of Saturday afternoon together that people only do after they have been together for years. We felt strangely comfortable. I say 'strangely' because I had never really felt comfortable on a date before. I had always had my barriers up. But now the combination of his sensitivity and the fact that I had grown to love myself made me really believe that what we were feeling was genuine.

Reader, you'll be glad to know that it was. We spoke to each other almost every day from then on and after a month, we had an amazing conversation about how we were feeling. I explained that I felt we were a really good match and he made it clear that he felt the same way. No more non-committal situationships. Alan and I were on the same page, looking for something similar in our lives and happy to feel like we may just have found it with each other. I was in London most of the time then and I would stay at his house after work every day. I had to be a little bit shifty as I hadn't told my parents about us (which I don't recommend) and I imagine my parents thought it was a bit strange how much time I was spending with my 'friends', but in time I built up the courage to tell them about us. When he came to visit they loved him straight away and any worries I had about them letting him stay over or me staying at his were unfounded. Parents can be very liberal when they see that their daughter is in a good place.

So in a good place we stayed. Throughout the first lockdown, we were house-sitting for his sister and by the second we had a chance to move in together at my family home. My parents were moving to Northern Ireland for work and asked me if I would move home to take care of the place (I'm not saying they didn't trust my younger siblings but . . .). I immediately said I would do it if Alan could move in and without a second's hesitation they agreed.

During that time, we began to work together more closely and more effectively, filming and editing every day, making our own couple's videos for YouTube and settling into the pattern of a mature, committed relationship. I think finding that security really helped me as I tried to find success in my work. It is a funny cycle – finding love helped me to be better in my career but it was the fact that I had already decided what I wanted to do and grown as a person that had allowed me to find love. I had to develop a strong, positive sense of my own identity before I was really able to let someone in, and that had come through dedication to my creativity and self-love. As a result I learned to love my work and myself more than ever, while I loved someone else.

Which brings us back to the focus of this chapter, the loving roots of fearlessness and the fearless foundations of love. My struggles to find a match were as much about myself as they were about anyone else. I needed to know my worth and appreciate myself before I could really let someone in, and I am glad that I didn't have relationships before I had learned those lessons. A relationship that starts from a place where you don't value yourself, where you think you are lucky just to be there, is built on unsteady foundations. People too often accept treatment that they don't deserve because they don't believe they deserve better. I know it because when my self-esteem was low I was happy to take any attention that would come my way. That is no way to build a partnership. Find a positive relationship with yourself first and *then* let someone else join.

So be patient, love yourself and wait for someone who finds joy in the same things that you do. That simple approach should be enough to help you get to the fearlessness that true love requires – even if it wouldn't make a very good pop song.

LOVE YOU

Wait, wait, wait to find another,
If you go straight, straight, straight to any lover,
Who has some trait, trait, trait that you've discovered
You liiiiiike (that's fetishising)

Girl love, love, love your very self
That's above, above, above everything else,
Just stay, stay happy on the shelf,
Don't build your love from your insecurity (that's
*   never vibin')*

Cos in time, time, time, you'll find the one,
Who loves you like you love you hun,
And you won't, won't feel the urge to run,
From that good place, new space in the sun (a new
*   horizon)*

OK, I take it back, maybe it could make a good
song. Someone call Cardi B.

The Timbo Takeaway

Most people want to be loved. Often, when we cannot find the love we want, we wonder what is wrong with us or what we lack. The truth is that we need to focus on what is right with us and what we have before we can be ready to give and receive love. Because the first loving relationship that defines all of the others is with ourselves. It can be hard to always have that love for ourselves if we have not always received love from family or friends, but in those cases, we have to separate our own perspective from those of others and build.

I used that basis of self-love to help me overcome the challenges I faced when it came to romantic relationships, and it gave me the strength to be patient, the security to overcome disappointments and the willingness to give everything when the right person came along. Who 'the right person' is will depend on you but remember that physical attraction is just one component. Your partner should be your friend and someone you would be happy to live with and give your time to even if you were not romantically involved. In turn, your partner should treat you the same way.

Remember that you are more than your best or worst attributes. You deserve to be loved. And the best way to show others how to love you is to model it by loving yourself.

Reflections

Write down three things that you love about you. These should be things that are not necessarily visible to people on the outside. They should be things that you are better placed to understand than others because you know yourself the best.

1. ....
....

2. ....
....

3. ....
....

Look back at the beginning of the chapter where I was talking about love languages. What do you think are the ways that you naturally show your love for people (family, friends or partners)? How do you appreciate them showing their love for you?

Think about someone you love. How do you think they like to be shown affection? Could you provide them with something meaningful to make them feel loved?

THE MOST IMPORTANT RELATIONSHIP WE HAVE IS WITH OURSELVES.

COMMANDMENT 9:

Be Heard

It is hard to thrive in a world that doesn't seem to respect people like you or listen to your perspective. But just because it's hard, it doesn't mean it's not necessary, and just because they don't listen, it doesn't mean that you won't be heard.

If this book has served its purpose, you should be feeling pretty fearless right now. You should trust in your ability to rise above the haters, to believe in yourself when the going gets tough and to reach out to the world and people around you with love, strength and curiosity. That is good but it's not enough, because true fearlessness is not just the absence of fear or doubt, it is the presence of strength – and that strength is what we all need to change the world.

Yeah, I know, maybe changing the world wasn't necessarily in your calendar this week. The invite has come at short notice and you might prefer to RSVP 'maybe'. I understand that. If you would rather sit at home eating ice cream and scrolling through socials (I recommend @fatstimbo) then we can consider that part of the plan, because this chapter is about what we do when we feel ready to change the world and the steps that we take to get to that place.

If you don't feel like changing the world right now then I can only think of two reasons why that might be.

1. You think the world is just fine as it is.
2. The problems are too big and/or you are too small to make a difference.

So let's deal with those in order.

In response to point number one, I have to say, *really?* Have you turned on the news (OK, me neither, but I still get a sense of it)? War, climate change, discrimination, it's all there to see. So my top tip for those in group one is to take a look around and see if there are any issues we might be missing. If you find them and still feel like there isn't anything worth changing, maybe consider the possibility that you are in group two but just need some time to think.

If your response was number two, that you aren't enough to make a difference, then I have to say that you are right, but not for long. And that's just because to change the world you really do have to believe in yourself; you have to trust your perspective and your right to share it. It is only by believing that you can make a difference. Sometimes, it is actually the process of starting to believe in yourself that brings about the changes you want to see. In my life, I realised that I was making a difference simply with my presence, by being unashamedly and proudly *me*. I saw that believing in myself was a matter of changing the world because the world that I lived in didn't make space for people like me to be confident and outspoken, so by speaking out confidently I could break that expectation.

Growing up, the only little people I saw in popular culture were a myth or a joke. I mean that with all seriousness. We were either playing magical creatures or providing punchlines. That was a challenge. Did I see myself through the lens that culture was giving me and, even worse, did everyone else? It was one thing to deal with my own self-doubt that came from portrayals of little people, but it felt too much when I considered how they made other people think about me. It made me uncomfortable because when everyone expects you to be a caricature, showing up as a complete person can be hard. So I had a choice: I could either stay out of the way, hope to avoid any of the flak that might come in my direction and live a quiet life that I did not want to lead. Or I could lead the life I wanted. I could be proud, I could be whole and I could be honest. It wasn't a matter of deciding to change the world, it was simply a case of being confident to be myself when the world didn't encourage it. I had to jostle for a place at a table that had no space for me and then demand an accessible chair (not too high, good back support, maybe some wheels if we are feeling jazzy).

I didn't want to be a pantomime performer, a fetish or a sidekick, but I don't necessarily blame anyone for making the world a place that expected me to be one. Those beliefs and behaviours go so deep in our society that it can be hard to convince people otherwise with words or theory, so my only option was action. For example, I appeared on *Good Morning Britain* in early 2022 to discuss a controversy around the representation of little people. The actor Peter Dinklage (Tyrion in *Game of Thrones*) had publicly questioned certain aspects of the upcoming *Snow White and the Seven Dwarfs* film. The film-makers had been very keen to shout about how this was a progressive take on the old classic, with a Latinx lead and an empowering female-led storyline. Dinklage's argument was that it could hardly be that progressive if it featured seven dwarfs working happily in a mine with paper-thin personalities that seemed to centre on a single trait (grumpy, happy, etc.) and I agreed. Part of the reason that I agreed was the same reason that I love Mr Dinklage – he is an actor with achondroplasia who plays roles that are not defined by his disability. He plays normal human beings with qualities and failings like the rest of us, with storylines not only centred on his disability and he can act *both* grumpy and happy depending on the situation. I think we can all agree that it is not ideal to have people with achondroplasia (or anything) defined by their condition or simplified down to singular character traits.

But what's that I hear you say? The Seven Dwarves don't necessarily have achondroplasia, they are magical creatures. Thank you for pointing that out, as it leads to my next point, which is . . . **Dwarves are magical creatures and people with dwarfism are normal human beings**. We have an issue because society uses the same word to describe people with a disability *and* creatures from fairy tales and there is not much room to separate the two. That creates the difficult situation where a child goes with their parents to see a pantomime and watches a series of comedic dwarves constantly being presented as jokes, then goes out into the world where their parents tell them to treat people with achondroplasia entirely seriously. They have just spent two hours laughing at the little people alongside hundreds of others and ten minutes later, they are being told that the little person in the street shouldn't be laughed at. I mean, how hard is that for a child? We either need to stop having little people play dwarves or change the name of the mythical creature. Simple.

Anyway, long story short, I made that point and I got a fair bit of flak. There were jokes flying around on social media about me and people calling me a woke warrior and a killjoy, and it felt *GREAT*. Because being an annoying little person who speaks their mind and disagrees with you in public is far better than being a joke or a fantastical being. I was myself. I had an opinion that people disagreed with and they didn't like me. Fabulous. Let's agree to disagree, just don't be surprised if I manage to be happy as well as grumpy, bashful, dopey or erm . . . sneezy about it.

You see, that is a clear case of how being yourself is enough to change the world. Anyone who called me a woke warrior was recognising me, defining me by my ideas and not my condition and quite possibly feeling that about a little person for the first time in their life. By being myself proudly, I was changing perceptions of people I had never met. Now I'm just sitting here waiting for them to make the live-action *Rumpelstiltskin* movie. I'm ready.

The great thing about changing the world by proudly being yourself is that you win both ways. You are benefiting both yourself and the world, and by doing yourself justice, you can move some of the way towards achieving justice for others. You might say that I'm oversimplifying it. That believing in yourself and just being yourself is much harder to do than it is to say, and I agree. It didn't take me a sentence or a chapter or even a book to get to a place where I valued myself enough to be myself, but positive words of affirmation really are a great start. My parents were the ones who instilled that in me. If you haven't got that sense yet, then maybe my words can help to instil it in you. If you are different then you are different, but you are not less than anyone else. We discussed in the first chapter how boring the world would be if everyone was the same, and how matching people's expectations is a recipe for disappointment. You have to think about who you want to be and if that doesn't fit with any mould that society has created for you then you have to ask whether you really want to try to force yourself into another shape. It might seem like fitting in is the easier option in the short term, that being the straight guy, the stereotype of a Black woman or the unassuming caricature of a disabled person will allow you to lead an easy life, but it won't. You are simply saving everyone else the trouble of having to adjust their expectations and you will never meet your own. This 'easier option' will be harder in the long run.

As the proud, authentic version of yourself, you will have taken your first steps to changing the world and I bet that it will give you the confidence and belief to move on to the external challenges. That brings us to the flipside of thinking you are too little to make a difference, which is believing that the problems are too big. My answer in that case is that it depends on the task you choose. We have just seen how doing yourself justice can be a recipe for changing the world and I think that points to a simple truth – you can take on a challenge of any size and you will have done something to be heard. The task may be small or large, personal or public, relatively simple or earth-shatteringly complex, but it still counts. With that in mind, it becomes clear that we are wrong to say changing the world is too big a job because it can be as small a job as you choose it to be.

In fact, I recommend starting with a small change. Once you have focused on building that secure base of self-love and pride in your authentic self, the next step is to look for small manageable changes that you can make. This has the benefit of giving you some practice and experience of the positive feelings that making a change can give, and there is always the potential for it to grow organically into something bigger. I really like the example of Franziska Trautmann (@ecofran) to illustrate this. When she was in college, she was drinking a bottle of wine with a friend. They decided to check whether the bottle would end up being recycled or go to landfill. They realised then that Louisiana, their state in the US, didn't actually have any recycling facilities for glass. Then and there they decided to do something small and they made a GoFundMe page to try to raise enough money to buy a single glass-crushing machine. That machine would allow them to crush glass into sand, which could be used to help restore the coastline in their local area. They got the money and there was some publicity around their effort, so people started delivering their leftover bottles to the backyard where they had set up the glass-crusher. With each delivery of leftover bottles they grew their operation – adding more glass-crushing machines and getting more people to send their recycling. A couple of years later, their project @glasshalffullnola is now operating out of a warehouse. They have recycled over a million kilograms of glass and work with scientists on cutting-edge projects to restore coastlines that have lost sand to erosion. What started with an idea over a glass of wine became a backyard project and then grew into something that changed their community. Even better, other young people have been inspired by their work and are setting up similar projects in their areas.

This is an example of how a big problem can be faced by starting with small steps. If you had said to Franziska before she began, 'I want you to process a million kilograms of glass and start a grass-roots movement,' she might have replied that such a task was too big. But by starting small and growing, Franziska was able to achieve something beyond her expectations. So if you are worried that something is too big a task for you, remember that you can start small and let your capacity grow at a pace that doesn't feel like too much. The task is as big as you choose it to be.

It's not just in activism where we can see that great things have small beginnings. Apple, the multibillion-dollar, world-changing, iPhone-dropping megacorp, started in Steve Jobs' parents' garage. Two dudes in a poorly lit room probably didn't seem world-changing at the time but it was. One of my favourite charities, PEAS,[3] started when a British teacher and his Ugandan friend decided to fundraise to improve a school building in Kampala. Now that charity educates over 15,000 secondary school children a year, with a focus on ensuring at least 50 per cent of their students are girls. You can start small and do huge things.

It is also important to remember that we don't have to go it alone when trying to change the world. All of the examples I have given so far involve pairs of friends working together towards a common goal, but there is just as much good to be achieved from joining a community as well. Sometimes, a project can seem too much to start alone, so look for like-minded people who you can see making a difference and join them. You

---

3 https://www.peas.org.uk/

want to improve the lives of disabled people in the UK? There are activist groups for that. You want to stand up for women's reproductive rights? There are activist groups for that. You want to make your community greener and fight the climate crisis? There are activist groups for that. By finding a community, you can add momentum to a movement that is already in motion and do your part, but, more importantly, you can develop connections and friendships that make the process enjoyable. I've found that having other disabled people around to talk about our shared experiences has been really powerful, helpful when things are hard and a source of extra motivation when I am trying to stand up for something. By working together, we create energy that is more than the sum of our parts and we can confront challenges that we never could as the same number of individuals.

So let's recap. If we want to be heard, first we need to learn to love the sound of our own voice, to trust it and believe that others will benefit from it getting louder. When we have developed that self-love and trust we can confidently present our true, authentic self to the world, which is our first step in making it change. Then we step out into the world to make the changes we want to see. This is a process of identifying, prioritising and collaborating. We need to choose our field (because we can't change everything at once), decide on a small, manageable course of action to get us started and then find people to work with to multiply our impacts and lighten our load. At this point, we need to decide on our platform, how we raise ourselves to make our voices heard and encourage more people to join us in our aims. This platform should be relevant to our work, our skills and our audience. For example, it might be that entering the political system is a way that some of us can achieve our aims, but in my case, running to be the MP for Ilford might not be the best use of my time. It may be for you. Do it. I'll vote for you. I have a platform already made on social media and opportunities to work on traditional platforms as well to communicate with even more people – so I am going to choose broadcasting as a way to share my message.

My choice of platform also reflects one of the aims of my activism because I want to see better representation of disabled people in entertainment. That means I can both raise awareness of the issue and counteract it by being present. I need to create a space in which I normalise capable little people appearing on our screens (as more than Oompa-

Loompas or munchkins), while at the same time demanding that space be opened to other people. I cannot stress enough how important representation is in this case. Growing up without any cultural reference points in terms of my disability – no musicians or presenters, comedians or cultural critics – I was taught that the world couldn't accept me as I was. On the other hand, I saw lots of examples of people who looked like me being figures of fun; entirely unserious people who didn't really have their own voices but played the fool in response to able-bodied characters who had complex personalities, character arcs and stories. So by representing, I am *representing* and I know how much of a difference that can make because I have felt it. When *EastEnders* introduced the character of Donna in 2014 it was a game changer for me. A little woman who wasn't defined by her disability appeared on national TV for four years. She was genuinely normal and that was extraordinary. So I want to provide a similar example to the next generation and, in the process, demand that this be the last time we have to force our way in.

I think a big change in representation will come as more disabled people are employed in the cultural sector, and this actually speaks to the second aspect of my activism. I don't just want to see more disabled people in entertainment, I want to work towards more professional opportunities for disabled people in all of the fields in which I work. The disability employment rate is about 30 per cent lower than that of able-bodied people, so there are hundreds of thousands of people who could benefit from more inclusive hiring policies. I think this is vital and as my platform grows, it is something that I will try to encourage across the board. In the short term, I'm focusing on entertainment as I already have my foot in that door and also because if more disabled people are involved in the production process, I believe we will see far fewer stereotypes and two-dimensional versions of disabled people ending up on screen, which will have an impact on how the next generation sees themselves. It is a big task, but it feels manageable because I know I can be myself, build from a platform where I feel comfortable and work to bring in other people who can multiply my impact.

The reason I feel comfortable with this approach is that my base is secure but I have no limits. This is what we discussed in terms of starting small but aiming high. In other words, I know that, at the very least, if I can be true to myself then I have succeeded but, equally, there is no ceiling to what can be achieved further along. I look at the example of what Rihanna did for the beauty industry with her Fenty range, and I believe that I can start small and still aim to achieve something similar for inclusive fashion. For those of you who don't know, Rihanna created a beauty brand that offered make-up for a wider variety of skin tones and palettes and in the process she changed a whole industry. I would like to work on something similar with an adaptive clothing range or through the creation of customisable fashion which can be adjusted at source to fit different body shapes. Rihanna saw that the beauty industry wasn't meeting her needs and acted on it, and I see similarities in fashion for disabled people. If I can use my platform to make a change in how the fashion world accounts for people with different bodies, then I will be proud to have created authentic action out of my own experience and by learning from someone else's efforts.

Which brings me to another important point in our discussion of fearlessness and change-making: don't be afraid to learn from others. Take pride in following a path that has been forged by your heroes and know that you can stand on their shoulders to reach even higher. It can be frightening facing up to the world on our own, but if we have examples of people who have done it before us, we can take strength from their achievements and learn from their methods. We can collaborate with the past if we are willing to learn from it and if we do, then we can create our own future.

After we have empowered ourselves by using the examples of others as a source of strength and a point of reference, when the time comes, we can in turn empower others. When we have become fearless and sought to change the world through our actions, we can be a source of fearlessness for those who come after us. When you can be a mentor you should and when you can use your platform to help others up you must.

If you want to know why I have written this book, there you have it. I would like the story of my own journey towards fearlessness, towards activism and being heard to become something that encourages you on your journey. I have been blessed with the support I need to stand up and stand out and I hope my words make you feel supported too. You deserve to be fearless and others deserve to benefit from the good that your fearlessness brings.

I hope I have helped in some way to show you how.

The Timbo Takeaway

To speak up, we must be fearless but to be fearless, we really have to believe in our right to be heard. That is why changing the world starts with believing in you. So you must know yourself and love yourself, and be brave enough to share that with the world, because that is your first step towards changing it. The process of coming to know yourself should then lead you to see what you want to change out there. It could be anything – but decide on what is important to you and where you think you have the energy and capacity to make a change. By working out what you want to change (e.g. the climate) and where you want to focus (e.g. fashion) you will have both content and a context that matters to you and you will find it easier to focus and stay on track if the going gets tough.

When you have decided on your focus, start small. It can be intimidating to try to take on a big problem from a standing start, so find those things that you can do and do them.

Taking these small steps can help you develop a platform and discover people to collaborate with, which will extend your reach and provide support along the way. Your collaboration may be in a team of two, or two million, but it is always easier to achieve change in a network.

Finally, remember to look for inspiration in others. Even if you are alone on your journey now, there are footsteps in which you can follow and trailblazers from whom you can learn. Trust in the example of your idols and take strength from them, and when the time comes, be prepared to offer your services to others who are just beginning on their journey to being heard. Be ready to follow and to lead, but be true to yourself as you do either. Have no fear because you are enough.

Reflections

Is there anything about you that the world struggles to accept? Do you hide it? Can you share it?

What issues do you want to confront in the world (e.g. climate crisis, discrimination, poverty)?

What fields would you enjoy working in (e.g. academia, business, sport, fashion . . . *anything*)?

When you put these two things together, can you see a way to work in a field you enjoy while making a change you want to see?

Find an example of an activist who has made a difference. What can you learn by researching their methods and approach?

....
....
....
....
....
....
....
....
....
....

TRUE FEARLESSNESS IS NOT JUST THE ABSENCE OF FEAR OR DOUBT, IT IS THE PRESENCE OF STRENGTH.

AND THAT STRENGTH IS WHAT WE ALL NEED TO CHANGE THE WORLD.

COMMANDMENT 10:

Look Back

and

Then Forward

Because both learning and dreaming are time well spent.

It's funny how the same actions can have such different impacts because of their intent. For example, looking back on our life can be nostalgic or a learning experience depending on how we approach it – and our intent can transform a moment of sadness spent dwelling on what we have lost into a moment of presence in which we learn from the places and people we have been. It all depends on how we do it. I think it is the same for thinking about the future. We can look forward and catastrophise – by focusing on some imaginary worst-case scenario and ruining the moment we are in as well as any chances we have to approach the future positively. We can wish time away – by imagining a future so perfect that we would do anything to speed our lives towards it, sacrificing our present. Or we can think about the future proactively, considering what we want and how our actions in the now are impacting our ability to make it come true. In all three of those situations, we are doing the same thing but how we are doing it has the power to create entirely different outcomes.

I want to talk about what I have learned from looking over the past in this book and discuss the future that I want to write into the next one – but, more importantly, I want it to provide an example of how we can look forward and back in a way that gives us strength and motivation. I want to make the past and the future contribute to our present because, really, they are both just the present in disguise.

What are you on, Fats? 'The past and future are just the present in disguise'? Have you become a wizard?

Good question. No, I haven't become a wizard, I'm just feeling a little bit philosophical as we reach this book's ending together. Or is it a beginning? Maybe it's a beginning disguised as an ending. Maybe I'm a wizard disguised as a TikToker. OK, that's probably a bit much, but I feel that the point about the reality of the past and the future stands – even if it sounds strange at first. The past is just a name we have for a present that has already been and the future is just a name for a present that is coming. We may put a sepia filter on the past to make it look like it was another world, and we might make everything look shiny and techy when we create images of the future, but that just disguises the fact that these were or will be someone's present. They might be yours.

I always notice the strange presence of the past when I see old videos that have been colourised. If you haven't seen them before then search them online. They are films taken by early video cameras that captured black and white footage but, using new technology, they have been made to appear in colour. When I watch them there is this strange realisation not just that the past really *happened* but, moreover, that it was really *happening*. The people you see on that screen were not living in the past, they were living in a very real present – going to work, meeting friends and trying to get by. So I try to keep a sense of the present when I think about the past and I think that helps me to approach it in a balanced way. Thinking about the past is useful if it brings joy or perspective to our present moment, but any time spent thinking about it negatively is really a waste. I'll say the same for your future: think about it optimistically and use that thinking to inform your actions in the present moment.

Don't live for it – but reserve an optimistic space for it in your present mind.

On that theme of keeping our past and future in our present minds, let's look back over what we've talked about in this book first and then discuss my plans for the future as well as think about yours. The first lesson I learned in my life and shared with you is that it is a great thing to be out of the ordinary. Although it can be hard to live outside of people's expectations, it is even worse to ignore your own. While it took me a long time to accept that, through years of staring and strange questions which created a desperate desire to be normal, I came to understand that normality never could or should be my path. So if you feel different, remember that makes you the same as everyone else – you have just admitted it to yourself and now you have a head start in living up to it.

We also talked about the importance of keeping those who give you love close. It is a powerful thing to be loved and it is something you deserve – so reserve your patience for the people who love you and will stand beside you in the long term, and show your best self to those who would love you even if you were at your worst. For me, the love and support of my family has been the base that

I build from, always, and even when the world outside seems cold and disappointment has come my way, I have always been able to return to the pillar of strength that they provide. Even if they can be *annoying*.

The strength and continuity that I drew from my family as a young person was one of the things that helped me get through some of the most difficult years of my life and retain my sense of self-worth when people tried to make me feel worthless. We discussed how to deal with bullies and haters in chapter three, and I hope some of my learnings from that chapter have stayed with you. It's so important to remember that people who want to bring you down are often doing it because they feel low themselves and pulling you down towards their level feels easier for them than pulling themselves up. That can be so hard to keep in mind when someone bullies you. The temptation is always to see their position of strength when they pick on you, but it is so important to see it as a mark of their weakness. Strong people don't bully people, only people who have been unable to overcome the pain or bullying that they have experienced do. Pity the person who bullies you because it is a sad thing to be bullied but much sadder to become a bully. If you can do that, then you can stop the chain of hurt that your bully is trying to strengthen and you can provide a release of the pain that exists in the world. Rising above the haters isn't just a neutral thing to do, it is a powerful act of kindness that you offer to the world, so be proud when you do it because you've just done something for yourself and everyone else on this earth.

I know that can be hard when other aspects of your life are tough. When the journey feels like a struggle, the idea of making an extra effort to ignore people who want to make it tougher can feel like a superhuman effort, but you have to remember that often the hardest things are the ones that give you the most progress. So trust your journey, like we talked about in chapter four, and see your hardships as a part of life's rocky road (*mmm . . . rocky road.* If you haven't had rocky road, try it. It's basically every sweet thing combined into a lump and I'm there for it).

There have been so many points when nothing seemed to be going to plan for me, my main character energy was depleted and I just wanted to go to the home screen and find a cheat code that would let me skip to the next level. But that's not an option and, even if it was, then I wouldn't advise you to take it. Sometimes the hardest parts are the most meaningful; they are the bitterness that makes the sweet (*mmm* . . . OK, I'll stop) so satisfying. What may seem like the hard part now may seem like the good times one day, so find the joy in there and remember other times in the past which you now feel grateful for.

Those hard times will also be more enjoyable if you keep faith in yourself – your self-belief. We talked about how the only thing worth doubting is your own self-doubt and I believe that deeply. Don't use your precious energy for doubt: put it all into doubting your doubts because they do you no good. If you believe in yourself you can put your energy into what you want to happen, rather than what you worry might not, and your chances of creating your ideal future will grow. Try it now. What do you want to achieve? What are your doubts about yourself or your ability to achieve it? Now doubt those doubts – question and undermine them. Treat your inner doubter like one of the haters in chapter three, feel pity for that side of your mind and tell it not to worry – you're not needed here today. It sounds so simple but it works.

The power that comes from stepping outside of

your self-doubt and treating it like a bad friend is one of perspective. When our doubts come from deep within us they feel like secret truths, but with a small shift we can see them as something more like bad advice or a friend who isn't really there for us. Our self-doubts aren't necessarily true or very well informed, they just feel like that when we fail to step away and look at them from another angle. This is the power of a changed perspective, which is also something we can gain from leaving the space that we are in. Our challenges can appear very different when we go to a new place and look back at where we were – we see that they seemed large because our perspective is small and that in fact they are a feature of a particular place and mindset. If we leave those things behind, often the troubles go too, or at least reduce. Travelling can also introduce us to other people's challenges, which is really important if we feel stuck or struggling and remind us of the size of the world and its opportunities.

Travelling also has an incredible way of making us stop and appreciate the moment. When we are caught up in our daily routine, it can feel like we have to go at a hundred miles an hour just to make it to the next day. As if our diary on any given day is all-consuming and requires us at full capacity.

It is only when we stop that we realise how we may work better and live life more fully if we take a moment to look around. That has always been true for me. Learning to stop and appreciate the moment, to see all the good things that I am taking for granted at any given time, has always helped. It is necessary because we are often so fixated on our destinations that we don't see the journey for what it is. *Everything*.

Finally, we spoke about the importance of love, particularly for ourselves, and how it forms the basis of any effort we make to change the world. It is only when we are kind and loving to ourselves that we have the strength and security to help others through their pain or to stand up for the things that we believe in. There *will* be disappointments and criticism when we do and your relationship with yourself must be secure to overcome them. When you look at your past with forgiveness and your present with kindness and patience, trust me, your future will look brighter and the bumps in the road will seem more manageable.

Which brings us to the second half of this chapter. We have looked back so now let's look forward. My hopes for the future probably won't be a surprise to you! You know the journey I have been on and hopefully I have made clear what is important to me, so I bet you can predict a number of the things that I want to achieve.

The first of which is . . . *world domination*. Fats action figures, a Marvel movie and presidency of a Global Government by 2026. I'm joking of course (though if you believed that maybe I should have considered putting in a chapter about staying humble!) but there is a bit of truth in that statement. I do want to do some big things. I want to break into television, presenting and hosting programmes of my own. In particular, I would love to make a series that discusses disability from a West African and a Western perspective, comparing them to show the surprising similarities and unexpected differences. I also feel like I am close to making a breakthrough with sketch and stand-up comedy. For a long time, people have been thinking about how we can get more of the great internet comedians a platform on TV and I think that I can help make that happen. My generation doesn't see our favourite comedians on television and I think we can change that. I need to keep working on myself to do this. I am challenging myself to do stand-up comedy and get more comfortable performing in front of a crowd because I can see it is an area in which I need to grow if I'm going to be a live performer and visible presence on live TV.

Why do I want those things? That is an important question and one which you should ask yourself when you think about what you want to achieve, because often we carry the weight of dreams that we haven't properly thought through. There are two reasons why I want to achieve a public profile and, in particular, become a face on TV. The first is simple: I am driven but I also want to be able to give back to my family and professional success will give me what I need to help them all, particularly my parents. My mother and father sacrificed a lot to give me the life and opportunities that I have had. They left their families and dropped their own plans by the wayside to be in a place where the next generation could thrive. Who knows what my life would have been like if they hadn't made some of the sacrifices that they did? All I know is that I want to help them so that they don't have to make any more. I want to be their retirement fund.

More importantly, though, I want to grow my profile because my existence is political. Every time I am on a TV screen, showing up for my disabled queens and telling my story, owning my narrative, I am taking a small step towards making the world more equitable for the next generation of girls like me. When my career finishes, I want to leave the entertainment industry a better place for disabled people than the one that I arrived in. One aspect of that will simply be a matter of turning up, being visible and doing my job well, but I will also have to be prepared to speak my mind. While a lot can be achieved by showing more disabled people on television, the next step will be for our voices to be heard. When we get in the room we need to be comfortable to share our perspective, to let writers and directors know when their depictions of disabled people are inaccurate or when examples from our lives could help make their creations more realistic. If we can do that as on-screen performers and also lobby to have a more diverse workforce behind the cameras then entertainment has the potential to make a big difference to the lives of disabled people in the future.

My hope is that by getting my foot in the door and being on the TV and radio, I can be part of a growing movement that is demanding people with disabilities be given opportunities to work in the entertainment industry, and the support and pay they deserve and need to stay in it. This is important on a couple of levels. One we spoke about – by being part of the conversation about how disabled people are depicted, we can make sure children don't grow up in the position I did, only seeing disabled people on television when they are either silent or a joke. The second aspect of it is that the disability unemployment rate is always far higher than the general unemployment rate, so I want to constantly use my platform to lobby for more opportunities. If I am working in entertainment, then I want to make it happen in the entertainment industry; if I'm doing a series about sports and leisure then I want to lobby for more gyms to employ disabled members of staff; if I'm at the MOBOs it will be the music industry. I want to be in the room so that I can hold open the door for more of my disabled brothers and sisters, wherever we may be.

If I can leave my career having helped my family financially, opened a few doors for disabled people to enter the entertainment industry and, as a result, improved the way we are presented in the British media, I'm done. Thank you very much. It's been a hell of a ride. I know what I want to achieve and I know why. The rest is a matter of how and when and any professional uncertainties that remain are the fun part.

In my personal life, the uncertainties are maybe slightly less fun. For example, I would love to get married and have children but I have to be conscious that my physical situation does make that complicated – not the marriage, the having kids. The make-up of my body means that there is always a chance that having children will be too dangerous or challenging. I have to be prepared for some difficult conversations and changes in plan on that front. I know that whatever I do, it will be the right thing for me, my body and the children that I do or don't have. I know Alan would love kids. He's lost both his parents and would be such a great dad, so the idea of starting a family is really powerful to him. I'm not in a place where I am ready yet and there is plenty of time, but I know whatever we do, it will be done with our health and the happiness of those children in mind.

Before that, I do want a big ol' wedding though. Because I am channelling some serious main character energy, I want it to be huge. I want it to be in a beautiful destination and I want it to go down in every guest's mind as an iconic event. That might be a bit much to ask, particularly the destination bit, so I will probably have to budge on that. It's not always right to expect people to spend time and money travelling to your wedding far away, so I think I might have to keep it in the UK but go big on the lavishness. It's a one-off (I hope) so I might as well go all out. In short, all I want is a beautiful summer wedding that is undoubtedly the biggest and best that every guest has ever been to. Is that too much to ask? My apologies in advance to the wedding planner.

So what about you? As I have said before, this book is as much about you as it is about me. How do you look back and forward in your life? How do you tell your story? If you look back and write your story optimistically and conscientiously, then your present and your future will most likely look the same way. So I have to recommend that you make an effort to narrate your life positively. There are two ways this can be done. One is to focus on the lessons learned from the hard times – because if you can't help but dwell on them then try to see what they taught you and what you gained. The other is to try to always be conscious of your style of narration. The South American writer Gabriel García Márquez once said, 'What matters in life is not what happens to you but what you remember and how you remember it.' It feels like that sums up what I am trying to say. Life is as much a story that we tell ourselves as it is something we do. I don't want to get all English Language GCSE on you, but life is not a verb, it's a noun, a thing. Living is what we do; life is the story that we tell ourselves. So we have to try to tell the story in a way that makes the living part enjoyable.

If we can do that, if we can learn from and appreciate our past and see that our present is a process to be enjoyed, then we can make our future into anything we want. So be present, be yourself and remember how lucky you are to be alive. We started this book with a conversation about my unexpected arrival in the world. What we didn't discuss was how little would have had to change for me never to have made it – a complication in the pregnancy, a surgery that happened too late, some bad luck. I was lucky to be born and so were you. So let's treat everything that comes afterwards, our whole lives, as a celebration.

Have a little dance. Sing a song. Eat some rocky road. Maybe tell someone you love them. Change the world. Because even if your past has been difficult, and your future looks challenging, it is a privilege to be existing in the present between them.

The Timbo Takeaway

Remember your past with a smile or learn from it. Enjoy your present and don't forget how strange and brilliant it is to be alive. See your future for what it is – another present that grows out of the one you are in now. Start living like it is your ideal tomorrow today.

Remember that in all of history (millions of years) and all of the known universe (millions of planets) you are one of a very small group of people who are alive right now. That is nuts. You've won the lottery just by being here – so treat life like one of those giant fake cheques that they give lottery winners. Hold it up, spin it round, admire it.

Enjoy.

Reflections

Look back on your past. Try to recall some good times that you may not previously have remembered in that way. I'm not talking about the obvious good times, like birthdays or holidays, I mean walking to school with a friend or waking up early on a Saturday to watch cartoons. Pick five ordinary times and see how extraordinary they were.

Look back on your past again. Remember the hard times. Pick five, maybe the ones you tend to dwell on, and then think about what you learned from them. Would you be the person you are today if you hadn't had those difficult experiences? Maybe you learned about resilience or the value of kindness. Maybe you learned about how important it is not to be cruel. Note them and see the positives in them that you may have missed.

Think about your future. What would you like to accomplish? What can you do now to make that come about?

Think about your future again. How would you like to experience it? Imagine all of those accomplishments if you didn't learn to enjoy the moment. Would they even matter? Think about the mindset you will need in that future present to make it enjoyable. Try to apply that mindset to the moment you are in.

....

....

....

....

....

....

....

....

....

....

PS. I said in chapter one that I would tell you why I twerked on a police car. The truth is, I've waited this long to tell you the answer because . . . I don't really know why. It was Notting Hill Carnival, I was pumped up on Soca and Supermalt and I saw that police car as the stage I needed and deserved. So I popped one foot up on the bonnet and I twerked. Enthusiastically. I do not advise that behaviour. The Metropolitan Police discourage it (although they haven't said that officially). I do not regret it. I'm older now though, so I will probably never do it again.

YOU HAVE TO REMEMBER THAT OFTEN THE HARDEST THINGS ARE THE ONES THAT GIVE YOU THE MOST PROGRESS.

ACKNOWLEDGEMENTS

I want to thank my family for making me who I am today. Your unconditional love is my secret ingredient. You taught me when I needed to learn, believed in me when I started to doubt and trusted me when I risked it all. I couldn't ask for anything more.

My friends, for always making me laugh and helping me to cry when I needed to.

Nora and Ciara at TMA, for being my champions and my defenders, for seeing my talent and knowing that it could take me further than even I believed.

To my co-writer Oscar Millar, for listening so carefully and telling my story so beautifully.

To the team at Bonnier and Blink Publishing. You helped make this dream a reality. You really are the best in the business.

To Alan, for your love.